YOUR PRODIGAL CHILD

YOUR PRODIGAL CHILD

Dr. D. James Kennedy
with
Norman Wise

THOMAS NELSON PUBLISHERS
Nashville

Published in Nashville, Tennessee, by Thomas Nelson, Inc., and distributed in Canada by Lawson Falle, Ltd., Cambridge, Ontario.

Printed in the United States of America.

Library of Congress Cataloging-in-Publication Data

Kennedy, D. James (Dennis James), 1930-
  Your prodigal child.

  Bibliography: p.
  1. Problem children.   2. Parenting—Religious
aspects—Christianity.   3. Intergenerational relations.
I. Wise, Norman.   II. Title.
HQ773.K46   1988   649'.153   87-31496
ISBN 0-8407-7619-5

1 2 3 4 5 6—92 91 90 89 88

CONTENTS

ACKNOWLEDGMENTS

This book is the result of the efforts of many. It would be impossible to thank all of them. However, special thanks must go to Karen Helder, director of Professional Services of Wedgewood Acres Christian Youth Center, and David Harvey, acting chairman, Department of Education, Geneva College, for their professional input in the manuscript; Jerry Newcomb, Coral Ridge Ministry staff member, who researched numerous books and articles on the subject; Nancy Britt, who read and gave her comments on the manuscript; and Janet Thoma, Thomas Nelson Publishers, who edited and re-edited the manuscript.

1

Can Anyone Help Me?

I rarely answer incoming telephone calls, but I was alone in the building before office hours, working on Sunday's sermon. The answering machine began to recite, "We are sorry, but no one is in the office . . . ," when, for some reason, I decided to interrupt the message and take the call.

The woman's voice was abnormally high pitched, probably from anxiety. "Oh, Dr. Kennedy, our daughter, Sue, is living on the beach in Fort Lauderdale. My husband and I watch you on television every Sunday and are always inspired by your messages. We've been so worried about Sue. We thought we couldn't do anything about it. Then we remembered that your church is in Fort Lauderdale. We thought, well, maybe . . . Could someone there help her?" The mother's voice had broken several times during her explanation. Now she began to sob.

We get many calls like this one from Katie Triner at the counseling division of the Coral Ridge Presbyterian Church in Fort Lauderdale, Florida, and at my radio and television ministry. Our counselors also answer hundreds of letters from parents who need counsel, because their children have run away or become involved in wild lifestyles.

"I can understand your concern about your daughter, Katie. We will try to help her. Remember, God cares for

Sue. Both of us need to pray that He will use this difficult time in Sue's life to help her recognize that her only hope is in Him. Try not to panic, and continue to commit your daughter to His care."

"Oh, Dr. Kennedy, I do trust in God, and I have prayed for Sue. But she is in more trouble than just leaving home. She's been on crack cocaine for over two years. Just five months ago, she entered a drug rehabilitation program. We were hoping that she'd be well again.

"But the moment she was released, she announced, 'I'm going to Florida. Don't worry about me. I'll make it on my own.' She called last night to tell us she was all right. 'I'll be sleeping on the beach,' she said, 'until I find a job and get a place to stay.' We're so afraid for her. Yet what can we do since she refuses our help? Can you contact her and see if she will accept help from you or the church?"

I knew from years of counseling that there are never easy answers to questions like Katie Triner's. At this point I needed some crucial background information if I was going to be of any help, so I asked, "Does Sue have any faith or religious training that might cause her to be open to our counselors?"

"We always went to church," Katie began. "My husband and I have raised five other children, all of whom are Christians. But Sue never had any deep faith. Once she became a teen, she began running around with a wild gang and soon became involved in drugs. She continued to live at home after she graduated from high school, but she had a hard time holding a regular job. She spent most of her money on drugs and booze. Sue has training in the Christian faith, but she has never applied it to her life."

Katie Triner and her husband are like thousands of other parents throughout our land whose children are living unethical and destructive lives. These parents feel frustrated and guilty. They are worried, anxious, and often at the point of despair. These natural emotions often keep them from getting help to learn how to reach out to their prodigals.

I have counseled both parents and prodigal children during my twenty-eight years as senior pastor of the Coral Ridge Presbyterian Church. Sometimes a counselor is able to intervene in the prodigal process and help the child and the parents. Other times our efforts seem to have little result. Sue Triner, Katie's daughter, had mistakenly thought that winters in Florida were like summers in the northeast; therefore, she was not concerned about sleeping on the beach or roughing it for a while. In fact, she thought this would help her to "become more resourceful" and even more of "her own person."

However, even Florida gets cold in winter; temperatures can drop as low as the forties at night. Sue became desperate for shelter. Her street "friends" had stolen her suitcase which contained all her personal items and extra money.

Cold and hungry, Sue decided to break into an empty house for shelter. Her sleep was disturbed by a policeman's flashlight. She was arrested and charged with trespassing and burglary. One of our youth counselors finally located her at the Fort Lauderdale jail. He spent time talking to her in her cell and then explained her situation to the local authorities. Yet when Sue was released from jail, she went back to the street, to drugs, and to wild living.

The many times I have had to tell parents, like the Triners, this disheartening news has led me to see the need for a book to provide practical and scriptural help to hurting parents whose children have strayed from their parent's faith and ethical values. Precious little seems to have been done to provide usable resources to teach parents how to effectively deal with their children and the emotional upheaval caused by their lifestyles.

A letter from a close friend of mine and a fellow minister added to my resolve. "Both of our children, Jim, have strayed from the Lord," he said. "Though I am a minister and my wife and I sincerely tried to raise them in the fear and admonition of the Lord, they have rejected the orthodox Christian faith.

"As my wife and I struggled with this reality, I became convinced that there must be others in our congregation who suffered the same problems but were afraid to discuss them for fear of embarrassment or condemnation. After much prayer my wife and I shared our personal hurt with our congregation and set up a time of prayer and discussion for other parents."

The response was overwhelming. The minister and his wife found that many of the parents harbored tremendous guilt, and they mistakenly felt that they faced this problem alone. Soon the couple established a parents' group within the church, "Concerned Parents," to meet the emotional and spiritual needs of parents in their community.

Recently, I heard from another friend that knew of several homes of full-time Christian workers where two or more children had rejected the faith. In a type of prodigal "chain reaction" these godly parents had seen their teenagers turn against them and their values. Such problems are not rare throughout our society and the Church.

DO YOU HAVE A PRODIGAL CHILD?

Webster defines the prodigal as "a person who wastes his means." In this book I will use the word in a much broader sense. The prodigal son in Jesus' story and the millions of prodigal children who inhabit our world are not just wasting their financial resources, but their very lives. They have left the ethical values of godly homes to adopt unbiblical beliefs, worldly values, and harmful lifestyles. These children are prodigals, whether or not they ever leave home, as Katie Triner's daughter did.

Adult children can also be prodigals. Frank, a middle-aged adult, lives with his parents because he is unemployed, even though his father continues to use his contacts to get him job interviews. Frank's dad has repeatedly loaned his son large sums of money for promising business ventures, which always turn sour. "Not because he hasn't tried to make them go," Frank's mom quickly assures other family members.

Frank's dad is usually more realistic. He knows Frank has a problem and often wonders, *How did we fail him*? Yet he refuses to admit that his son has an alcohol problem and is immature and unstable. Frank has never sought professional counseling. Because of guilt, Frank's father continues to loan him money. He's afraid that Frank might commit suicide if he were kicked out of the house and forced to support himself. Although Frank is an adult, he is, nevertheless, a prodigal.

Frank and Sue are prodigals, just two of thousands of children who have abandoned their parents' beliefs to adopt destructive lifestyles. Many of us realize how common this problem is in our country because we know prodigals within our immediate circle of family and friends. The frightening statistics of alcohol and drug abuse, children born to unwed mothers, and teenage suicide rates show the increasing number of prodigal children in the United States:

• Teenage alcoholics are a primary concern of high school counselors, since 92.6 percent of high-school students have used alcohol.[1] Teens are also using illegal drugs in growing numbers; 54.9 percent have used marijuana at least once and 16.1 percent have tried cocaine.[2]

One in ten teenagers smoke marijuana on a weekly basis and three in ten report getting drunk once a week. Two out of five have used an illicit drug besides marijuana.[3]

• One million teenagers will become pregnant this year, according to some estimates, with half of those conceptions ending in abortion.[4]

At the present time, one out of every ten teenage girls are becoming pregnant. Four out of five of these pregnancies occur out of wedlock. Nearly 30,000 of these pregnancies are among girls who are under the age of 15. If the current trend continues, experts estimate that 40% of all 14-year-old girls now living in the United States will become pregnant at least one time before the age of 20.[5]

Births to unmarried women in the United States hit an all-time high in 1985, accounting for 22 percent of all live births, according to the Department of Health and Human Services. This figure represents a 24 percent increase over 1980.

Unwed women twenty-five and older had the greatest increase, accounting for 30 percent of out-of-wedlock births in 1985.[6] This statistic reflects the current attitude among young women who want a career and motherhood, but not marriages.

More than 70 percent of our teenagers will have sexual relations before the age of twenty.[7] Josh McDowell, a leading Christian youth specialist and author, states that his research indicates that 60 percent of all Christian teens have had sexual relations.[8]

• Approximately one thousand teenagers a day attempt suicide, according to Jerry Johnston, a counselor who has spent years researching teenage suicide. Johnston says that males are much more likely to kill themselves than females.[9]

• Ninety-six percent of teenagers leave the church within two years after graduation from high school, according to a recent survey commissioned by a major conservative evangelical denomination. Less than 30 percent ever return. Many of our children simply end up without any strong religious beliefs.[10]

Young people surveyed by George Gallup, Jr., and Jim Castelli in March of 1987 said that religion was less important to them than to their parents by a margin of two to one. Religious faith was listed as last in a list of eight values that were important to young people.[11] In broad sociological terms, this generation of young people is turning away from the faith of their fathers.

Statistics like this cause some parents and ministers to give up in despair. Yet there is hope. Consider this story of a famous prodigal who was raised by a Christian mother and a hedonistic father. The boy, we'll call him Allen, was sent away to private school until he was sixteen, when his father could no longer afford the tuition. Allen returned home and that year ran with a wild gang in his hometown.

Although he returned to private school the next year, he continued to drink and party. Soon he met a beautiful young girl and after several months of going together, she became pregnant.

Allen had attended church as a child, and he sometimes tried to read the Bible when he felt discouraged with his reckless lifestyle. The book always seemed, "Too stuffy and irrelevant to my life," he told his mother. Still he enjoyed the writings of Plato and other philosophers. After he graduated from school, he became a professor at a well-known university. This young man was so much of a prodigal that some Christians felt it a useless waste of time to attempt to call him to the faith.

Mothers like Allen's have become legendary. Praying

mothers, we call them. No matter what her son did, Allen's mother continued to pray for him and faithfully attempted to influence him to return to the Christian faith. Her quiet reminders of God's will for his life finally convinced him to break up with his mistress of ten years and to look for a wife. Just when his mother thought he might be settling down, Allen took another mistress.

Still his mother continued to pray.

Allen began reading certain books by Christian writers and slowly began to sense the Holy Spirit within himself. He tried to return to the Christian beliefs of his childhood, but he was unable to stop drinking or to give up his second mistress. Again he turned to the Scriptures for help.

The words of the apostle Paul, "For the good that I will to do, I do not do; but the evil I will not to do, that I practice," (Rom. 7:19) truly described his dilemma. As he read further in Paul's writings Allen began to see the grace of Christ, which is available to any man in his weakness.

One day Allen was sitting in the garden, reading the Scriptures, when he was convicted by Paul's exhortation to the Romans: "Let us walk properly, as in the day, not in revelry and drunkenness, not in licentiousness and lewdness, not in strife and envy. But put on the Lord Jesus Christ, and make no provision for the flesh, to fulfill its lusts (Rom. 13:13–14).

"I was filled with a light of certainty," he later told his mother, "and all shadow of doubt disappeared."[12] His mother's faithful and diligent prayers had been answered.

This brilliant scholar shaped Christian thought for generations to come. The man's name? Augustine, Bishop of Hippo (A.D. 354–430). Without doubt he was one of the most influential Christian theologians of all time. Yet, he was once a prodigal.

Every generation has its prodigal children. Augustine in A.D. 400. The prodigal son in Jesus' time. The boy next door or your own daughter today. Parents are often heartbroken when their child rejects Christian beliefs and values, yet they need to understand that the prodigal process does not have to end in tragedy. Many times this process brings a person to a deep belief in God.

In this book I will examine this prodigal process, which occurs in stages, just as any developmental process. Each chapter represents a stage in this process, and each chapter answers the questions parents most often ask me or our counselors at that time.

I will show how the parable of the prodigal son in Luke 15 can be a model for parents to use in responding to their child's prodigal behavior. Most chapters will begin with a short fictional dialogue between the parable's characters. The prodigal son, I will call "Produs"; his father, "Theo"; and his elder brother, "Judd." The dialogue between the prodigal son and his family will suggest the particular phase in the prodigal process considered by that chapter. We will also look at other examples of prodigal children in the Bible to help us understand how much influence Christian parents can have upon their children.

Throughout this book I will use stories of parents and their prodigal children based on true accounts (names and circumstances have been changed) to illustrate positive strategies for coping with today's prodigal children. This book is written primarily for parents who have teenage children, but it also contains useful insights for those who have adult prodigals and for parents of younger children who want to begin early to do all they can to keep their children from becoming prodigals.

The book will help you to think through what steps parents can take to prevent having prodigal children, how to handle the emotions of having a prodigal child, and the best method of being used by God to reach your prodigal for Christ. It is my prayer that this book will help parents struggling with the prodigal process by giving them concrete answers to the questions that arise from having a child turn away from faith and home.

Many parents are praying for their prodigals, as Augustine's mother did, and many of them live to see miraculous changes in their children's lives. For the rest of his life, Augustine proclaimed, "O Lord, I am Thy Servant, and the son of Thy handmaid: thou has broken my bonds in sunder. . . . Let me know thee, O Lord, who knowest me: let me know thee, as I am known."[13] Augustine's mother could not ask for a more miraculous answer to her prayers. Neither can we.

2

Am I to Blame
If My Child Is a Prodigal?

July 10, A.D. 30

Dear Diary,

I am so concerned for my son, Produs. He does not seem to be interested in the affairs of the farm. His thoughts are always on the life of the city. I have had to be quite stern with him because of his laziness and impulsive decisions. I fear that he lacks any true belief in the ideas and values I have tried to teach him. In fact, if he were outside the restrictions of our home, I'm afraid he would quickly get involved in serious transgressions of the law.

Theo

Sunday morning at the Harrison's house had become just one more skirmish in the continuing battle between them and their twelve-year-old daughter, Linda. Thirty minutes before they were to leave for church, Linda would come down the stairs still dressed in her pajamas. This particular Sunday morning she walked slowly over to the

17

television, flicked on the switch, adjusted the dials, and then strolled over to the couch and sunk into a comfortable position.

Helen Harrison, Linda's mother, was sitting at the kitchen table, watching Linda's actions. Since Linda obviously intended to watch television, Helen asked, "What are you doing, young lady? You've been awake for the last forty-five minutes. Dad and I thought you were getting dressed for church."

Linda glanced toward her mother, then back at the television set. "I told you I don't want to go to church anymore. Why sit on those hard pews while some old man tells me that having a good time is wrong? I don't need church."

The Harrisons could not understand Linda's attitude. They had taken her to church every week for Sunday school and the evening service. They had sacrificed to send her to a Christian school and had encouraged her to attend activities at school and at church.

This morning, Ralph Harrison overheard the argument as he came down the stairs. "You don't need to go anywhere else this week, either. Be ready to go to church in ten minutes or you are grounded. It's your choice."

Linda knew better than to argue with her dad. But, even though she went to church with her parents, she was silent and obviously angry. The Harrisons were praying that her attitude was only a stage in her development. "She will outgrow it," they hopefully told each other.

During the next several years, the Harrisons continued to spend time with Linda. They took bike trips with her and attended her school play and piano recitals. Ralph and Helen tried to be consistent in their Christian lives. They also talked to Linda about their faith. Both of them participated in our Thursday night evangelism outreach program.

Yet Linda withdrew emotionally from them. She spent much of her time alone in her room; the hugs and kisses she used to give them, just for being "mom and dad," became infrequent, a grudging response to their affection for her.

The year Linda became fifteen, Ralph and Helen began to suspect that Linda and her best friend were skipping Sunday school to walk down to the local ice cream store. During the family worship service, Linda would often close her eyes, yawn, and doodle on the bulletin to demonstrate her boredom.

One day, Ralph received a call from Henry Townsend, the principal of Maranatha Christian School. Before the principal could say anything, Ralph asked, "Is everything all right? Has Linda been hurt?"

"Well, Ralph," Henry Townsend responded, "that's a good question. You see, Linda has not been in school for three days. This morning, when she finally showed up, she handed her teacher a note from Helen, saying that she had been sick. But Linda didn't show up for her afternoon classes. Her teacher thought she might have become ill again, so I called your home. No one answered."

That night Ralph and Helen confronted Linda. Ralph threatened her with every punishment he could think of and grounded her for two weeks.

"I'll run away," Linda threatened. "No one understands me. You, the school . . . everyone punishes me."

After this fight with her dad, Linda seemed to give up any attempt to please her parents and teachers. She refused to study or turn in her homework; she skipped classes. She started disrupting classes with talking and horseplay, and she was caught smoking in the girls' bathroom almost daily. The school counselor and her parents attempted to show her that her actions were only hurting her, but Linda would not listen. Except for short bursts of anger and rebellion, Linda refused to talk with her parents, teachers, and counselors. Finally, the school principal asked Linda to leave, "for the good of the rest of the students."

THE STORY OF THE PRODIGAL SON

Where can parents like Helen and Ralph go to find guidance? For hundreds of years the story of the prodigal son, found in the fifteenth chapter of the Gospel of Luke, has proven to be a classic tool to explore the prodigal experience.

While Jesus' parables were never based on one specific individual's experience, they were always woven around experiences that were common to people of the day. Many people were shepherds so Jesus told the parable of the lost sheep to help them understand how God felt when someone rejected Him. Farming was another prevailing occupation so it became the basis of the parable of the wheat and the tares. Obviously prodigal children were also common in Jesus' day.

A parable always illustrated truths about the kingdom of God. In this case, the father's response to his son was the same as God's response to any of His prodigal children. Jesus also implied that fathers should respond to their children as God responds to them. For this reason, I will use the parable of the prodigal son as an example of parenting and talk about this father and son in the light of the Hebrew culture of the time.

Jesus didn't tell us much about the son's actions until after he left home, but we can imagine that the son's unusual request for his inheritance was preceded by some other rebellious actions. Indeed, our minds conjure up quickly the image of the father who has spent years worrying about his youngest son.

The father Jesus described would have done everything

to raise his son to love God and follow His ways. The major concern of Jewish parents in biblical times was that their children come to know the living God. In Hebrew the verb "yada," *to know,* means not only having intellectual knowledge about a person but to be intimately involved with a person. Godly parents helped their children develop a relationship with God.

A godly father in a Jewish society would also have followed the advice in Proverbs to "train up a child in the way he should go" (Prov. 22:6). He would have talked to his son about Yahweh as they sat in the house and as they walked together in the fields. A mezuzah, containing God's words about raising children (see Deut. 6:4–9), would have hung on the doorpost of his house to remind the entire family of their responsibility to God.

Imagine this father's pain when his son left home and spent his inheritance in a depraved lifestyle among unbelievers!

Ralph and Helen Harrison felt the same pain and fear as their daughter continued to reject them. Jesus' story of the prodigal is the logical beginning point for Christian parents looking for biblical models to help them through the prodigal process because it reflects the bitter realities of their own experience. Yet, Jesus' story gives hope even to parents who have tasted the bitterness of seeing their children become prodigals.

A FAMILIAR DILEMMA

When Linda graduated from high school, she celebrated her freedom by moving out of the house and taking an apartment with an older girl friend. Her mom and dad tried to visit her, but their visits always ended with a major confrontation. Finally, Linda and her friend moved to a new apartment without leaving a forwarding address. Like the father of the prodigal son, the Harrisons had no

The Parable of the Los

Then He said: "A certain man had two sons. And the younger of them said to his father, 'Father, give me the portion of goods that falls to me.' So he divided to them his livelihood.

"And not many days after, the younger son gathered all together, journeyed to a far country, and there wasted his possessions with prodigal living.

"But when he had spent all, there arose a severe famine in that land, and he began to be in want.

"Then he went and joined himself to a citizen of that country, and he sent him into his fields to feed swine.

"And he would gladly have filled his stomach with the pods that the swine ate, and no one gave him anything.

"But when he came to himself, he said, 'How many of my father's hired servants have bread enough and to spare, and I perish with hunger! I will arise and go to my father, and will say, to him, "Father, I have sinned against heaven and before you, and I am no longer worthy to be called your son. Make me like one of your hired servants."

"And he arose and came to his father. But when he was still a great way off, his father saw him and had compassion, and ran and fell on his neck and kissed him.

"And the son said to him, 'Father, I have sinned against heaven and in your sight, and am no longer worthy to be called your son.'

"But the father said to his servants, 'Bring out the best robe and put it on him, and put a ring on his hand and sandals on his feet. And bring the fatted calf here and kill it, and let us eat and be merry; for this my son was dead and is alive again; he was lost and is found.' And they began to be merry.

"Now his older son was in

Son

the field. And as he came and drew near to the house, he heard music and dancing.

"So he called one of the servants and asked what these things meant.

"And he said to him, 'Your brother has come, and because he has received him safe and sound, your father has killed the fatted calf.'

"But he was angry and would not go in. Therefore his father came out and pleaded with him.

"So he answered and said to his father, 'Lo, these many years I have been serving you; I never transgressed your commandment at any time; and yet you never gave me a young goat, that I might make merry with my friends.

But as soon as this son of yours came, who has devoured your livelihood with harlots, you killed the fatted calf for him.'

"And he said to him, 'Son, you are always with me, and all that I have is yours. It was right that we should make merry and be glad, for your brother was dead and is alive again, and was lost and is found.' "

Luke 15:11–32

idea where Linda was—or when or if she would ever return.

Three months later, Kelly, one of Linda's friends from high school, came to visit the Harrisons. For a while they chatted about Kelly's new job and the whereabouts of other classmates, but Helen sensed that Kelly's visit had a hidden purpose. Finally she asked, "Kelly, have you heard from Linda? Do you know where she is or how she is doing?"

"Well, I really came over to tell you that you need to try to reach her," Kelly admitted. "Linda has quite a reputation around town." Kelly lowered her voice and her eyes, as if she were afraid to tell the Harrisons anymore. Her silence seemed to reflect an inner battle between her loyalty to her friend and her concern for Linda. Finally she said, "Some of the guys brag about Linda's being an easy date. One of the guys says that he got her started on drugs and she's really hooked.

"I tried to talk to her," Kelly explained, "but she just wouldn't listen. I thought if you knew about this, you might be able to do something."

Ralph and Helen thanked Kelly for her concern and then wrote down the phone number and address where Linda was staying. It was too late to do anything that night, but the next day they would try, they assured Kelly.

At 3:00 A.M. they were awakened by the phone ringing. A male voice said, "This is Lieutenant Jackson. We have taken your daughter to Gordon Hospital. We found her lying on the street, badly beaten. The man she was living with apparently beat her up and left her there. Please come to the emergency room immediately."

As the Harrisons drove to the hospital, they tried to comfort each other. "The policeman said that Linda was not critically injured," Ralph reminded Helen. "Maybe God will use this incident to bring Linda back to us."

Linda was glad to see her mom and dad. She came home the next day to recover and for a while they enjoyed being together again. Slowly, however, the tension began to build as Linda stayed out late at night, all night, and then disappeared for days at a time.

One day they came home and found a note in her bedroom: "I have to be on my own. Don't worry about me. I'll keep in touch."

For the next eight years Ralph and Helen stood on the sidelines and watched a hopeless merry-go-round: Linda would bottom out, return home, regain her strength, then leave again to resume her lifestyle of sex, drugs, and booze. Finally, she was arrested for dealing drugs, convicted, and sent to prison.

The Historic Consequences

Again Ralph and Helen's story is not too different from the father's story in Jesus' parable. His prodigal son squandered his inheritance on wild living—gambling, drunkenness, promiscuous sex. And the results of this lifestyle were similar, too. The prodigal son also "bottomed out."

The son in Jesus' story ran out of money as a famine hit the land. His fair-weather friends deserted him. We can imagine him roaming the streets, looking for a job, his clothes becoming tattered and his appearance disheveled as weeks turned into months. He had not been trained to be a coppersmith, a merchant, or a lawyer, the professions of the city, and it is doubtful that he learned a trade after he left his father's house. The only job that he could find was as a servant for a landowner, tending pigs.

The prodigal son may not have ended up in jail, as Linda did, but his situation was just as degrading. The son obviously worked for a Gentile or an unorthodox Jew (an unfit companion, and never the employer of a self-respect-ing Jew), since they were the only people who raised pigs, which were ceremonially unclean. A Talmudic proverb declares: "Cursed is the man who tends swine, and the man who teaches his son Greek wisdom!"

The prodigal son soon came to envy these filthy animals. They had food to eat—husks, pods of the carob tree that were fodder for domestic animals and eaten by the poor in times of dire need. Yet the starving prodigal son would have gladly eaten those pods.

The prodigal son in the Bible, as prodigal children today, learned that a profligate lifestyle always carries a high price tag. Parents of these children also suffer from the child's actions. They cannot help but wonder, *What have we done wrong?*

What Have We Done Wrong?

Helen and Ralph came to me soon after Linda was expelled from Christian school. Many different strategies were used in an attempt to deal with Linda's rebellion. I suspected that Linda was only outwardly conforming until she finished high school, and I was right.

Often our counseling sessions centered around the guilt that Helen and Ralph felt. "We tried to be good parents, Dr. Kennedy, but we must have failed. Surely Ralph and I have sinned in some way to cause Linda to be this way. Maybe we should have been easier on her or . . . "

"Now, Helen," Ralph interrupted, "we tried being easier and that only led to worse problems. I feel that maybe I should have been more strict. Maybe I should have spent more time with her."

Now I interrupted. "Listen, both of you, it isn't going to do Linda any good for you to dredge through the past to discover every mistake you made as parents. If you have committed some major mistakes, admit them to Linda and ask for her forgiveness.

"But let me assure you. By all normal standards, both of you have tried to raise Linda in a godly manner. She has chosen to reject this teaching and she has to face that responsibility. You cannot accept the blame for Linda's actions."

Most parents who have prodigals ask the question, "What caused our daughter [son] to reject our faith and values? Did we do something wrong?"

The best place to look for answers to these questions is in the Bible. Although modern man dismisses religious faith as an "escape" from reality, Christians who read the Bible regularly know that the Bible is the story of real people with the same problems we face today. The pages of the Bible are filled with true stories of families who had prodigal children.

PRODIGALS IN THE BIBLE

If you begin at the beginning, you immediately read the story of Adam and Eve, the first children of God and the first prodigals in biblical history. God offered them paradise, a land He created specifically for them, free from death and decay. Only one commandment governed this perfect environment. God said, "You may not eat of the tree of knowledge of good and evil. If you do, you will die."

Still Adam and Eve turned their backs on God and ate the forbidden fruit. They chose to side with Satan in his rebellion against the Lord of the universe. (See Gen. 3.)

Did God do anything to cause their disobedience? No. He gave them a perfect place to live and He walked and talked with them in the cool of the evening. God loved His first children, yet they rejected Him.

Even when people are given a perfect environment, perfect instruction, and perfect personal commitment, there is no guarantee that they will choose to respond positively. This scriptural truth flies in the face of most "experts" of our day. Yet it goes a long way to explain why even the best programs with the best plans and more than adequate resources sometimes fail to help people. After all is said and done, each person is responsible for his or her own actions. He (or she) can respond positively or negatively to those who are trying to help. Children themselves must bear the brunt of their failure.

The Israelites' confusion about this issue can be seen in a proverb. "The fathers have eaten sour grapes, And the children's teeth are set on edge" (Ezek. 18:2). God told the prophet Ezekiel to order the Israelites to abolish this proverb.

Nearly 2,700 years ago Ezekiel explained to the Israelites that God's judgment is not based on our parents' failures but on our own failure to follow His Word. " 'Behold all souls are Mine; The soul of the father/As well as the soul of the Son is Mine; . . . The soul who sins shall die. The son shall not bear the guilt of the father nor the father bear the guilt of the son' " (Ezek. 18:4, 20a).

Ezekiel even gave the example of a son who has a sinful father. How does this son respond? He sees his father's wickedness and decides against his way of life. In this story the father is a prodigal, but the son decides to live a righteous life: he worships the Lord, feeds the hungry, clothes the needy, and helps the poor. (See Ezek. 18:14–18.)

No parent has ever caused his children to become prodigals. Though this truth is easy to grasp intellectually, parents like Helen and Ralph often have difficulty overcoming the guilt they feel. I often told them, "Look at the Bible. You'd expect to find perfect families there, but you will find many parents who had prodigal children."

MANY PRODIGALS, MANY REASONS

Faithful Abraham was the father of Ishmael, a wild man who was constantly in fights with his family and others. Isaac, the promised son given to Abraham by God, raised Esau who lacked faith and married a pagan wife. Jacob's sons sold their youngest brother, Joseph, as a slave to a caravan of strangers going to Egypt. The biblical list of parents whose children grew up to be prodigals goes on and on.

Out of all of these examples, two are particularly helpful in understanding what might cause a child's prodigal behavior. These two examples are: Samuel and his two sons—Joel and Abijah—and David and Absalom.

Samuel and His Two Sons, Joel and Abijah

Most parents hope to be as good an influence on their children as Samuel was. He wouldn't have been a father who said, "Go to church, it's good for you," and then remained at home. Samuel's life was dedicated to serving God as His prophet, priest, and a judge of His people. Since Samuel deemed it a sin not to pray for others (see 1 Sam. 7:5–8; 8:6), we can be sure that he prayed for his sons.

Since Samuel was a Nazarite, we know that he was not a drunkard, and he remained faithful to his wife. (The Nazarites took a vow of abstinence from intoxicating drinks and separation from sensual indulgence.)

We can also speculate that Samuel would have been a fair disciplinarian. Samuel is known for having "judged Israel all the days of his life" (1 Sam. 7:15). After the government of Israel changed to a monarchy under King Saul, Samuel still acted as a circuit judge, going from place to place giving divine judgment upon moral and spiritual questions and maintaining the law and authority of Jehovah. (See 1 Sam. 7:16–17.) His judgment must have been wise, since all Israel mourned for him when he died.

The only mistake that we know of that this wise judge made was to appoint his sons as judges to succeed him. Joel and Abijah took bribes and perverted justice. Finally, the people protested their administration. "Look, you are old," they said to Samuel, "and your sons do not walk in your ways. Now make for us a king to judge us like all the nations" (1 Sam. 8:4–5).

Imagine Samuel's grief and embarrassment. His sons' profligate ways were common knowledge to the people, yet he was unaware of their extortion. To be told in public, after a lifetime of worthy service, that his sons were unworthy, not because they lacked wisdom, but because they had disobeyed God's commandments, must have broken the old man's heart.

What had Samuel done to cause his son's thievery? Nothing, as far as we know. You might speculate that Samuel could have neglected his sons because of his political and spiritual responsibilities, but he was never rebuked by God for neglect as his mentor Eli was. (See 1 Sam. 2:22–36.)

Samuel was a good father. Yet his sons were prodigals. David and Absalom's story is far different.

David and Absalom

David is known as "the man after God's own heart." Who could have a better nickname? Often David deserved this title. His psalms of praise, worship, and meditation show the Godward direction of his life. His faith was also unquestionable. He defeated the giant Goliath when he was only a poor shepherd lad, with no weapon except a sling, and he gave God the credit for the victory.

At first David was a good role model. Then, when Absalom was growing up, David made a drastic mistake. His passion for the beautiful young woman, Bathsheba, caused him to disobey God's commandments. He not only committed adultery with her; he had her husband, Uriah, killed to hide his sin.

The prophet Nathan rebuked David. This led David to confess his sin and humble himself before God. "Have mercy upon me, O God, according to Your lovingkindness," he cried out. "I acknowledge my transgressions, and my sin is ever before me" (Ps. 51:1–3). God forgave him, but this did not blot out the impression David's action made on his third son, Absalom.

This boy was not too different from some prodigals today. One might call him a handsome wheeler and dealer. He rose early in the morning so he could stand at the gate of the city. When anyone came to bring a problem before the king, Absalom expressed his interest. "Look, your case is good and right," he would say, "but there is no deputy of the king to hear you. Oh, that I were made judge in the land, and everyone who has any suit or cause would come to me; then I would give him justice!" (2 Sam. 15:3–4). Time and again Absalom used such tricks to gain the people's favor and displace his father.

Earlier in his life, Absalom had murdered his older brother Amnon because he had raped their sister, Tamar. With Amnon dead, Absalom was the heir apparent to the throne and would have been king if he had been willing to wait. Yet he plotted to overthrow David, raised an army in defiance of his father's rule, proclaimed himself king, and attempted to kill his father.

Like most prodigals, Absalom finally "bottomed out." This young man who had a throne ready-made for him eventually met tragedy and disgrace. His army was defeated by David's forces, and as Absalom fled from David's soldiers, his long flowing hair, a symbol of his pride and vanity, was caught in the thick boughs of a tree. He hung there in midair until Joab, one of the commanders of David's army, thrust three spears into his heart. Absalom was buried, like a dog, in a pit in a lonely wood.

Some would contend that David's sins set a bad example for Absalom, and for that reason he failed to have proper values. However, Absalom was only one of several children. Though some, like Amnon, did commit grievous sins, not all of them became prodigals. Absalom chose to be influenced by his father's failure rather than by his repentance and his renewed commitment to the Lord. He alone was responsible for his actions.

NOT A CAUSE, BUT AN INFLUENCE

No one can deny that parents' actions do influence their children's behavior, but it is just that—influence. It is not a cause and effect situation, as a match set to a dry thicket causes a forest fire. David repeatedly forgave Absalom for his many sins, perhaps because David realized that his own sins had had a secondary impact on his family.

Adam and Eve also must take some responsibility for the actions of their son Cain. These first children of God, the first prodigals in the Bible, were also the first parents—and the first parents to experience the pain of having a prodigal child.

Their oldest son, Cain, became so jealous of God's response to his younger brother, Abel, that he killed him. While Cain must bear the primary responsibility for his actions, Adam and Eve's own rebellion set the stage for Cain's transgression. They are ultimately free from responsibility for Cain's actions, but they are not free from the responsibility for their own failure. Their sin probably had a negative effect on their son. Parents need to recognize that their own sins—and how they respond to them—can greatly influence their children's behavior.

We do make mistakes and sin against God, but we have a choice in such a situation, just as our children do. We can confess our guilt and seek the forgiveness of God and our children or we can try to hide our sin. Yet, whether we repent or not, we need to recognize our sins cannot force our children into a life of sin.

But Doesn't the Bible Say . . . ?

Some people resist teaching that prodigal children are responsible for their own sinful choices and that parents simply provide a positive or negative influence. They claim that the Bible teaches that people can "cause" others to become prodigals. They point to Jesus' answer to his disciples' question, "Who then is greatest in the kingdom of heaven?" (Matt. 18:1).

To demonstrate his answer, Jesus called a little child to Him. "Assuredly, I say to you, unless you are converted and become as little children, you will by no means enter the kingdom of heaven."

At the same time He warned them, "Whoever causes one of these little ones who believe in Me to sin, it would be better for him if a millstone were hung around his neck, and he were drowned in the depth of the sea" (See Matt. 18:1–7).

At first Christ seems to be saying that a person can "cause" a child to fall into a lifestyle of sin. In order to understand this discrepancy, let's look at the Greek word for *cause* in this passage: the word *skandalion*. In the context of Matthew 18, this word does not mean that a person actually forces another to sin, but rather that he can be a negative influence on another person's life.[1] The passage does not teach that parents are ultimately responsible for the sins of their children, but that we do have an influence on them. Our children, and they alone, must answer to God for the choices they make.

Does this principle exonerate parents who commit child abuse or raise their children in sinful environments? Of course not. Once I was eating dinner in a restaurant with my wife, Anne. I couldn't help overhearing the conversation at the table across from us.

The young boy (he couldn't have been more than five) was swearing and using foul language which had obviously been taught to him by his parents. The adults were laughing and suggesting new words, even more blasphemous, for the boy to use. *How can parents be so blind to their influence in that child's life?* I wondered.

Certainly God is troubled by abuses of parental responsibility, and all parents need to beware of falling into similar sins. God will punish us for our own sins but not for our children's sins.

What About Samuel's Sons?

What could have caused Samuel's sons to become prodigals? Yet another influence besides their home life—the pervasive influence of the culture around them.

Think about our own culture for a minute. Many factors are influencing our children to accept standards they might otherwise reject:

A lack of commitment to the marriage relationship.

There were 2.5 million marriages in the United States in 1986 and 1.2 million divorces. In fact, one out of every eight marriages in this nation will end in divorce.[2]

Adultery among married people is also common. It is now estimated that as many as 66 percent of all men and 50 percent of all women commit adultery sometime in their married lives.[3]

The lack of faith in marriage as an institution is seen in the increasing numbers of adults who choose not to marry.

Rev. Dick Purnell, who has ministered to singles in this nation for the last twenty years, estimates that the single adult population will soon equal the married population.[4]

Children today wonder, "Will my parents be the next to get a divorce?" They lack the stability in their homes that is needed for them to resist peer pressure. As the influence of the home declines the power of peer pressure increases. Unfortunately young people are greatly influenced by their peers. As Dr. Jason D. Baron, founder of Drug Abuse Programs of America has said: "Peer pressure is such a strong factor that it can undo the progress made in therapy in a very short period of time."[5]

Peer pressure is one of the major influences in children's decisions to use drugs and alcohol, and also is a contributing factor to their sexual activities. Among our youth culture today, one of the worst names a child can call another is "virgin."

Children are also familiar with the unusual marital situations of their friends' parents. Even ten-year-olds understand that the man who lives with Joanie's mom is not her husband, but a "friend." Since the child likes Joanie, she does not easily see her mom as doing something wrong, especially when Sally's mom and Jennifer's mom are also living with "friends." When the sociological norms begin to accept immoral behavior then children get confused about what is right or wrong.

A Lack of Moral Values

The secular view of life taught by the public schools and colleges adds to the basically amoral values a student sees. Traditional ethics are banned from the classroom, while the philosophies of ethical relativism, the sexual revolution, and humanism dominate the curriculum. Sometimes children are taught that their parents' belief in Christianity is simply a sign of their archaic and emotional outlook on life. They are assured Christianity will become obsolete in the light of modern science and open-minded investigation. The ethical standards a parent suggests are made to appear to be old-fashioned taboos which have no place in the modern world.

This materialistic and hedonistic way of life influences our children to think, *Nothing is right or wrong, black or white.* Many people in the United States make daily decisions without ever considering biblical principles. "What course will give us the most money, prestige, power, and pleasure?" many people ask. In such a society it is easy for children of Christians to govern their own choices by the same cultural values, totally ignoring the ethical and religious dimensions of life.

These factors cannot force our children to go astray, but they do provide powerful and pervasive temptations, which may be stronger than the influence of the home. Often the parents are only one influence on the life of a child, and in some cases not even the primary influence. We cannot isolate our children from the world. Negative factors will come into their lives which will tempt them to forsake our beliefs and values.

Some parents suffer guilt, even though they, like Samuel, have done little to cause their children to rebel. Even after I have given them the above explanation, they are still troubled by false guilt.

WHY ARE WE UNABLE TO REJECT FALSE GUILT?

At a deep emotional and intellectual level, most parents in Western civilization feel responsible for any failure their children experience. Children often reinforce this guilt. Ralph Harrison told me some of the things Linda said to them.

"If you and Mom weren't always cramming religion

down my throat, maybe I'd be more interested in God. You're so religious that I feel as if I'm living in a convent or something. You never let me have any fun—and then you tell me this is God's will. Sounds to me as if He's some universal killjoy."

Helen and Ralph were shaken by this accusation, especially since they were open to accepting the blame for Linda's behavior. Many prodigal children try to "pass the buck" for their bad decisions onto their parents. One young man, Dave, who had been convicted for a long string of burglaries and drug abuse, told his therapist, "My mom and dad fight all the time. They never have time for me. If they had loved each other and shown me some love, I never would have been in this mess. What do you expect from me? Look at the kind of home I come from."

Children have unconsciously, and consciously, learned to use sociological and psychological theories as manipulative tools to rationalize bad behavior and excuse themselves from accepting any responsibility for their actions.

David and Phyllis York have summarized this problem in their book, *Toughlove Solutions:*

Imagine the absurdity of a world where many people act like Geraldine, the comic character created by Flip Wilson. Raising hell until confronted, they say, "Well, don't blame me. The devil made me do it." Don't laugh. That absurd notion is contemporary reality among many professionals who work with kids in trouble. Every day young car thieves, vandals, burglars, and drug dealers are excused from real consequences for their crimes because they fit the popular psychological perceptions of the juvenile justice system. Every day some family therapists are telling parents that their relationship is the underlying cause of their child's unacceptable actions.

It is true, of course, that parents have a tremendous influence on their children. It is true, of course, that children are deeply affected by a father who molests them or a mother who abandons them. It is true, of course, that divorce can have a disruptive effect on a child's personal development. But ultimately we have to ask the question, "Who's minding the store?" Who inhabits that human body and determines what it does? Who or what steers its course? Some external force? Parents? Past events?[6]

As parents, therefore, we must recognize this popular belief sold to our culture that parents are ultimately responsible for the actions of their children as false. This misconception has loaded parents down with a crippling false guilt. Well-known child psychologist Benjamin Spock tells of a letter written to him by a mother who was frustrated by such imposed guilt trips. He later discovered this was felt by many other parents as well. She wrote:

> But don't you realize, that when you always emphasize that a child basically wants to behave well, and will behave well if he is handled wisely, you make the parent feel responsible for everything that goes wrong? Perhaps some people wouldn't get that feeling. But I do; and it is more burdensome and discouraging and oppressive than I can express. Can't you see that a parent is a human being, too?"[8]

This mother expressed the frustration felt by many parents in the last generation. Assured that good parenting would always produce good kids, they now have had to cringe in horror as their children have adopted ungodly lifestyles which, according to popular wisdom, could have been avoided if only they had been handled wisely.

When I was counseling Ralph and Helen, I told them, "You cannot accept the blame for Linda's actions—for your own sakes and hers. If she thinks she can make you responsible for what she has decided to do, she will be able to avoid the deep question of personal responsibility, which lies at the heart of her problem. We all make mistakes as parents, and we have to confess them. But false guilt and assuming full culpability for our children's sins is only going to lead to more problems and heartache for everyone."

Ralph and Helen and Linda are still in the midst of the prodigal process. Linda has not "come to herself," as the prodigal son did. However, Ralph and Helen have developed a strategy of working through their emotions and reaching out to their daughter, which I talk about in Chapter 8. They see the Lord giving them strength and guidance in the midst of their problems. Someday they hope to say, "Our daughter was dead and has come back to life! She was lost and is found!"

3

Does God Promise that My Child Will Love Him?

The letter written to me by a mother in Colorado was typical of many letters I have received. The woman described how her son had rejected the Christian life and through his wild lifestyle caused havoc in their family life.

"I just do not understand, Dr. Kennedy, why God failed to keep His promises to me and my husband," the woman wrote. "We did everything we could to raise our son in the faith: we lived godly lives, tithed, took him to church, made sure he was involved in the youth group, and sent him to a Christian school.

"But now we are faced with an adult son who is an atheist and refuses to even discuss the matter with us. If God failed to keep the promise He gave in Proverbs 22:6, then how do I know He will keep any of His promises? This question has torn my spiritual life to shreds and has thrown my faith into a sea of doubt."

Thousands, even tens of thousands, of Christian parents face this woman's dilemma. Not all blame God. Many blame themselves as I mentioned in the second chapter. "If I had raised John in the way he should go," they reason, "he would not have departed from the Christian walk. I've failed in my responsibility to God."

Unfortunately, parents accept Proverbs 22:6 as an absolute promise: "Train up a child in the way he should go, and when he is old he will not depart from it." Did God really mean it that way?

PROVERBS 22:6

Most young Christians are taught to learn the promises of God and depend on them. Charles Spurgeon, that great English preacher, once likened these promises to blank checks that only await our signature to be cashed. This counsel was wise and in accord with God's nature. He is a faithful God. If He has promised something, He will provide it.

However, most Christians have not been taught how to distinguish between an absolute promise and a general principle. Many people take a statement in the Bible and claim it as a promise when the author never intended it to be an unconditional guarantee of divine blessing.

We must always look at the context of the passage. The book of Proverbs, for instance, is a collection of short, pithy statements which express general truths or principles. What would happen if we attempted to make other proverbs into promises instead of general principles?

Let's try this with Proverbs 15:1, which says, "A soft answer turns away wrath, But a harsh word stirs up anger." If we take this to be a promise of God for every situation, we could expect that each time we gave a gentle answer to a person, his wrath would be dispelled. This principle might work for a while. That's the definition of a principle, "a basic truth or assumption."

One fateful day, however, our gentle answer would be met with hostility and anger. At that moment, we might say, "Wait a minute! Didn't God promise that 'a soft answer turns away wrath'? God isn't honoring His promises." Or, as the parents who accept the guilt themselves might say, "Well, I thought I gave Henry a gentle answer, but I must not have, since he yelled at me. I must strive to make sure that my words are truly gentle." The reality of the situation is that, even though we have acted correctly, others will sometimes respond with sinful actions.

All parents need to realize that God never intended Proverbs 22:6 to be a guarantee that children raised faithfully would be godly. In fact, the writers of Proverbs were fully aware that godly parents might have ungodly children or they would not have said: "Whoever loves wisdom makes his father rejoice; But a companion of harlots wastes his wealth" (Prov. 29:3). This proverb and others like it (see Prov. 2:1; 10:5) face reality: children can reject their parents' moral and spiritual training.

Proverbs also admits that children may curse their parents: "There is a generation that curses its father, and does not bless its mother. There is a generation that is pure in its own eyes, yet is not washed from its filthiness" (Prov. 30:11)

Children, according to the book of Proverbs, may also despise their parents (see Prov. 15:20) and mock them (see Prov. 30:17). Indeed children raised in a godly home may even be so heartless as to run through their parents' money (see Prov. 28:24) and to refuse to help a widowed mother in need of food and housing (see Prov. 19:26).

Proverbs portrays a realistic life in which good and bad exist simultaneously. After all, the writers of Proverbs were reflecting life as they experienced it (after man's fall into sin) and not a storybook existence. What then does Proverbs 22:6 teach?

WHAT DOES PROVERBS 22:6 TEACH?

If Proverbs 22:6 is not a promise, then what does it tell us about parenting? This proverb explains the parent's responsibility to dedicate his or her children to God and to train them in His ways.

In the original Hebrew, the phrase "in the way that he should go" reflects the thought that parents need to give consideration to the particular child's stage of development and unique personality. Rather than teaching that every child be fit into some legalistic mold, this verse urges parents to train a child to love God and serve Him in the light of the child's unique gifts and temperament.

Dr. Gleason L. Archer, professor of Old Testament and Semitic Studies at Trinity Evangelical Divinity School, summarizes the parents' duties and their realistic expectations in this way:

> This type of training implies a policy of treating children as even more important than one's own personal convenience or social life away from home. It means impressing on them that they are very important persons in their own right because they are loved by God, and because He has a wonderful and perfect plan for their lives. Parents who have faithfully followed these principles and practices in rearing their children may safely entrust them as adults to the keeping and guidance of God and feel no sense of personal guilt if the child later veers off course. They have done their best before God. The rest is up to each child himself.[1]

If we follow the advice in Proverbs 22:6, there is a good probability that the child will either remain true to this instruction all his life or return to God's teachings as he matures. This, however, is only a probability, not a certainty.

Some parents might continue to feel guilty when they read Proverbs 22:6 because they hear it saying that we can only expect our children to be converted if we are perfect in our role as parents. Such reasoning ignores the vast number of passages in the Bible that assure us that if we attempt to live a godly life, God will bless us.

God does not expect us to be perfect parents, only parents who try to achieve His goals for our children. He does not require perfect obedience from us since He knows this is impossible. If we do our best, we can be confident that He is pleased by our sincere efforts.

OTHER PROMISES GOD NEVER MADE

Sometimes parents quote other passages of Scripture to extract a promise from God that their children will either remain true to Christian principles or return to the faith. Some people think, *If only I had more faith, then my child would believe. After all, God said "Ask and it will be given to you; seek and you will find." It's my fault, because I have so little faith.*

Some parents attempt to use "praise power" to manipulate or force God to touch their children's lives. They stand up in prayer meetings and say, with great emotion, "Father, I praise you because you have saved Susan. I praise you because she is a believer in your sight. I praise you because she is your daughter. Please manifest this truth in her life so I might praise you for that as well."

Still other parents who are more traditional fall back upon the covenant promises of infant baptism. These parents maintain, "I had John baptized and made him a child of God. God never loses one of His children. He tells us this in the parable of the Good Shepherd. He must bring John to faith and repentance or He has broken His promise."

Each of these approaches assumes that finite man can force the infinite God to act. This is a misunderstanding of the relationship between God and man. Ritualistic views of God teach that the divine Spirit must respond to certain words and actions of man just as members of the occult and priests of primitive religions utter certain words and incantations to make their gods act. Abracadabra and your wish is granted!

Not so! Biblical faith is much more complicated than this abracadabra religion. The Christian God is the personal Lord of the universe. He is working out His plan of redemption through Jesus Christ according to His perfect will. God is sovereign in our salvation and He grants it according to His mercy upon whom He chooses (see Rom. 9–11; Eph. 1).

Yet, this Sovereign Lord can be touched by prayers of His people. God allows Himself to be influenced by our prayers, but He will never be forced to act because of our prayers. We need to hope that God will act, yet always be ready to accept His decision with a peace and submission.

As John White said in *Parents in Pain:*

> Your children can be given an understanding of the things of God however alienated from God they now are or may yet become. They can be given the capacity to see clearly. . . . It is for these things you may plead in prayer to God. They are your children's covenant rights. But you, as a parent, have neither the right nor the ability to control your child's destiny. It is a matter that will be resolved between your child and God.[2]

God intended parents to be a great influence on their children. Yet, we are not given the ability to predestine their salvation. Rather than struggling under false guilt or turning against God in anger, we need to trust Him and draw upon His strength if we are to help our troubled children.

If we don't, our prodigal children will see us struggling with unresolved guilt or doubting God's wisdom, and this will be a negative influence on them. Guilt and doubt interfere with the good influence we may have on our children in the here-and-now when we can still do something to point them to God. I believe that parents can fulfill their part of Proverbs 22:6 by accepting five specific biblical responsibilities.

FIVE AREAS OF PARENTAL RESPONSIBILITY

1. Prayer and Evangelization

Parents have the responsibility to pray for the conversion of their children and to teach them the gospel of Christ. In chapter six I will suggest a specific evangelism approach for parents to share with their children.

As soon as children realize that they do things that are wrong, they should be taught that they can be granted forgiveness for their wrongdoings if they accept Jesus Christ as their personal Savior and ruler of their lives. They should understand that a person is not saved because of good works. Rather, he is saved because of the mercy God manifested in Jesus Christ's suffering on the cross as payment for his sins. Not only is this correct theology, but it is also a proper foundation for the child's spiritual and emotional growth. This truth allows our children to accept less than perfection in their relationships with God and others. It delivers them from a lifetime of pursuing the impossible.

2. Godly Role Models

Parents have the responsibility to demonstrate a consistent Christian character in a life dedicated to the practice of love and truth. It will do little good to teach our children about Christian principles unless we are attempting to practice them.

This is why Deuteronomy 6:4–9, one of the most important parenting passages in the Bible, begins with a personal admonition to parents: "You shall love the LORD your God with all your heart, with all your soul, and with all your might. And these words which I command you today shall be in your heart" (vv. 5,6).

We must not communicate to our children the attitude of "Do as I say, not as I do." If we fail to practice Christianity in our daily lives, we will be influencing our children to reject Christ, rather than accept Him.

After Moses spoke about the parents' personal commitment to God in Deuteronomy 6, he gave the Israelites a plan for making their love of God a part of their everyday lives and the lives of their children. "You shall talk of them [God's statutes and commandments] when you sit in your house, when you walk by the way, when you lie down, and when you rise up" (Deut. 6:7).

God's principles were to effect everyday decisions. "Should our family worship an idol?" The answer was in God's Word: "You shall have no other gods before Me" and "you shall not make for yourself any carved image" (Deut. 5:7–8). Parents were to show by the decision they made and the guidance they gave their children that God's Word governed their actions. Parents were also to mention the principle that influenced each decision so the children would know how to make similar decisions in the future.

These parents were to tell their children about their Hebrew fathers—Abraham, Isaac, and Jacob—and to recall God's care of His people throughout the persecution in Egypt and during the long journey through the wilderness. Such a continual recounting of God's guidance builds faith: "God helped us in the past; He will help us in the future."

Moses further suggested to the Israelites, "You shall bind them as a sign on your hand, and they shall be as frontlets between your eyes. You shall write them on the doorposts of your house and on your gates" (Deut. 6:8–9). Moses suggested that the people write select sentences of the law upon their walls and the walls of the synagogue so that they would be reminded of these principles and their commitment to them.

Some people today make fun of "Jesus junk." And some of the items (like Scripture soap) that are sold in stores today deserve their derision. However, Moses' command to honor God's Word can be expressed in our homes by hanging a framed portion of Scripture on the wall of a bedroom or the kitchen to remind each family member of his commitment to the Lord. Each day he can judge his actions by that standard.

Other Christians I know write an inspiring portion of Scripture on a piece of paper and attach it to a mirror in their room or the refrigerator (the communication board of modern-day families) in the kitchen so that they can reflect upon its meaning. Moses suggested similar practices to the Israelites centuries ago as a way to "train up a child in the way he should go." This teaching was to be backed up by consistent ethical living and joyful participation in community worship.

3. Church Attendance

Parents have the responsibility to take their children to a church that is doctrinally sound. Such a church teaches the essential truth of the gospel of Christ and believes in the Bible as the Word of God. This church should also have an effective ministry to young people. A church like this is not easy to find, but its lasting effect upon your children makes it worth the time to visit many churches before selecting one rather than just joining the church closest to you.

Under no circumstances should Christian parents take their children to churches where the Word of God is rejected and a false gospel preached. Such an environment can be deadly. Children pick up a cynical attitude toward the Bible and Christianity that is difficult to overcome.

One of the main questions that is raised as our children grow older is whether or not it should be mandatory for them to attend church. Parents need to recognize that more damage may be done in the teen years by forcing attendance at worship services than by pointing out to the child that he should want to worship God. To be of value, worship must come from the heart. The prophet Isaiah warns Israel of a hypocritical worship, which is empty of any true desire to please God:

> When you come to appear before Me, who has required this from your hand, to trample My courts? Bring no more futile sacrifices; incense is an abomination to Me. The New Moons, the Sabbaths, and the calling of assemblies— I cannot endure iniquity and the sacred meeting. Your New Moons and your appointed feasts My soul hates; they are a trouble to Me, I am weary of bearing them. When you spread out your hands, I will hide My eyes from you; even though you make many prayers, I will not hear. Your hands are full of blood. Wash yourselves, make yourselves clean; put away the evil of your doings from before My eyes. Cease to do evil, Learn to do good; seek justice, reprove the oppressor; defend the fatherless, plead for the widow.
>
> Isaiah 1:12–17

It is important that we stress to our children that an empty, rote "churchianity" is useless; therefore, they need to seek a true and living faith in Christ. Our children must come to a place where they want to worship God and study the Bible if their faith is going to have any real impact on their lives. When they leave home to go to college or work, they will have that decision to make.

Ralph Harrison was right to want his daughter Linda, a cocaine addict, to attend church. However, parents need to avoid an open confrontation each Sunday morning. Ralph should have discussed the possibility of Linda's visiting another Bible-believing church if she wanted to change churches. And in the midst of this turmoil, her need to personally consider Christ should have been clearly stated.

This is easier to do if the child is reared with a family that has attended church every Sunday unless hindered by sickness. Even though the child may question this practice as a teenager, the years of church attendance will reinforce the parents' desires.

Watch out, however, for inconsistency. The parent who does not attend church with a child or skips church to play golf or allows the entire family to miss Sunday service during vacation is telling a child that there are exceptions to the faithful attendance rule. It is also important for parents to refrain from getting involved in church politics and to avoid having "roast pastor" for Sunday lunch. If our children see a loving community of Christians who experience the living presence of Christ, they will not be bored or inclined towards staying home Sunday mornings.

4. Relationship

Parents have the responsibility to attempt to develop a good relationship with their children. This relationship will include:

times of play	times of work
times of laughter	times of tears
times of listening	times of praise
times of encouragement	times of rebuke
times of teaching	times of hugging
times of conflict	times of forgiving

Part of committing our children to God is committing a major portion of our lives to them, according to God's will. After all, "We are His hands, we are his feet," as the familiar poem based on 1 Corinthians 12, reminds us.

Unfortunately, some parents have come to believe that the amount of time spent with our children does not matter. "It's not the quantity," these parents tell me, "but the quality of time together that matters."

All too many parents today seem to be practicing this idea and saying to themselves, *Even though I do not get to spend much time with my children because of my career, friends, and hobbies, I do devote quality time to them. When we are together, I make the time special, full of excitement and warmth. That's what really counts.*

My strong conviction is that you can't have quality time with your children without the investment of a quantity of time. As Jim and Sally Conway, experts in human development and authors of an article on creating family unity, said:

> People who film documentaries eventually learn that you can't do one without spending hours and hours of what seems like unproductive time filming ordinary circumstances. But in the midst of the ordinariness, in a totally unpredictable fashion, every once in a while a beautiful moment occurs. The same thing happens in family life. Spending time together allows quality to break through.[3]

If our children are still minors, they need our time. Good parents always guide a child who is changing and growing as an individual. Children should be taught and encouraged by parents but not smothered with over-protective fear. We must allow our children to grow up and assume full control of their own lives before God.

Yet, even when our children are grown, we still need to

give them as much time as their schedules and commitments to their own families allow. Children in the Bible looked to their parents for leadership until they became married or independent financially. Even when the children left home, they were required to give their parents proper respect and consideration. (See Gen. 2:23; Deut. 21:18–21.) Often the children, and even the grandchildren, continued to live with the father. The sons often worked with their father in his business as his assistants.

The Bible endorses the extended family as the best model of family life. By biblical standards, the small nuclear family seems hardly adequate to handle the hard trials of life. Not only do parents have a responsibility to their children all their lives, children have the obligation before God to help care for their parents as they grow older (see Matt. 15:1–6; 1 Tim 5:1–4). The family is bonded together "until death do us part."

5. Education

Parents have the responsibility to give their children the most godly education they can. This will usually mean sending them to a Christian school or teaching them at home. When a Christian school is not available or is beyond the financial ability of the parents, then public schools must be considered, but today only as a last resort.

Many will feel that I am being too critical of the public school system. Every location, of course, is different. There may be some areas of the country where the public schools are still providing a good education, disciplining effectively and motivating young people to accept traditional moral values. However, these locations are becoming fewer and fewer. A careful study of the public school system in most large cities will point out a growing inability to effectively educate children. This is seen in classrooms with declining discipline and curriculum introducing many unethical ideas which promote early sexual experimentation and drug abuse. Parents must make the decision regarding their children's education before God in good conscience. However, this decision must be made with a full understanding of what their children will learn and experience in the public school.

If children must be sent to a public school, the parents have the responsibility to take an active part in the PTA and to review the curriculum if possible. Since Christian parents may find themselves in the midst of controversy, they must be careful to try not to embarrass their children. But parents must also help their children to understand that sometimes embarrassment is a part of taking a stand for what they believe.

The children of Christians who attend public school should be taught to question teachings that are contrary to the Christian faith. Their publc education, dominated by a secular approach to life, must be supplemented by the home and a church with a clear understanding of a Christian perspective.

The great danger in sending our children to public schools is that secular and anti-Christian philosophy is taught and practiced. Some of the ways this philosophy manifests itself both in actions and words are:

- A growing amount of violence in public schools
- Low academic standards
- Acceptance of immoral sexual lifestyles in sex education
- Promotion of a secular, evolutionary explanation of life
- Promotion of ethical relativism
- The influence of many unbelieving peers

The public schools have become a gauntlet that would sorely test the morality of the best of saints if they were exposed to this anti-Christian environment eight hours a day, five days a week for twelve of the formative years of their lives. To place our children in such an environment is, in most circumstances, to place them in physical, emotional, and spiritual risk.

The secular university is even more dangerous, since many of a person's beliefs and values are formed during the college years. A proper college education should strengthen and encourage a child's faith (not attack it), which is the goal of education in a good Bible-believing, Christian liberal arts college. These colleges are listed in *A Guide to Christian Colleges* (Grand Rapids: Eerdmans). Your child should be encouraged to attend one of them. I believe that Christian parents should refuse to pay for a secular education in a university dedicated to a non-Christian view of life.

Sometimes our children's choice of occupation (in fields such as medicine, engineering, or another specialized or technical field) will demand an education that is not currently available at Christian colleges. In such a case, we need to encourage these children to attend a Christian college for the first two years and then complete their degree in a secular school, which excels in their chosen field. This background in Christian thought and apologetics is essential to a child's Christian life and faith.

Though this idea may seem radical to some people, I cannot over-emphasize the critical importance of a child's education. Computer experts tell us that a computer is only as good as the knowledge programmed into its memory. "If you program garbage in," they warn, "you get garbage out." This principle is all too true of a child's mind. If we place our children in an educational environment in which they are fed large doses of anti-Christian philosophy and psychology, we cannot be surprised if they eventually accept these views.

As I wrote back to that mother in Colorado, my eyes were filled with tears. I knew that her heart was breaking over her son's sinful lifestyle. I knew the agony she felt as doubts about Her Savior and His Word filled her heart and mind because of her wandering child. I assured her that even though she had no iron-clad promise, she could still have hope, for God has brought many a prodigal home.

4

Is My Child Becoming a Prodigal?

Memo

From: Produs

To: Dad

I want you to give me the inheritance which we discussed on an earlier date. It is about time you recognize that I am responsible enough to be given ownership of my share of the holdings. I no longer need you looking over my shoulder at every little detail. I would appreciate it if this transfer of property could take place as soon as possible.

> *Thanks,*
> *Produs*

Many people thought of the Suttons as the typical, wholesome American family. Fred and Marge Sutton were successful professionals—he, an engineer; she, an

56

accountant—who had a good marriage and were the faithful parents of two children, Tammy and Luke. The family attended church regularly, and although Fred's language was a little rough when he was upset, he tried to practice his Christian faith.

Then Tammy and Luke became teenagers. Tammy, the oldest, who had always been a good student, began to skip school. When Fred and Marge were aware of her delinquency, they reaffirmed the importance of an education and disciplined her.

One day, the principal, Mr. Talmert, called Fred and Marge. "Tammy has been suspended for two weeks," he said. "She and her best friend, Suzanne, were found drinking beer on school property.

"You should also know, Mr. Sutton, that I have talked to Tammy's teachers and discovered that she is failing several of her classes. We all feel that she needs counseling and help beyond what the school can provide."

Embarrassed, angry, and frustrated, Fred immediately phoned Marge and told her the story. She was able to cool Fred's anger by reminding him of the trouble he had gotten into during their high-school years. By the time Fred picked Tammy up at school he was calm enough to control his tongue. However, he could tell by the blank look on her face that she had either drunk too much beer to fully recognize the significance of her suspension or she just did not care.

Fred and Marge knew they were faced with problems at home, which would take a great deal of their time before any resolution could be reached. Yet their professional positions often required more than forty hours a week. They determined to spend whatever time was necessary since they knew they needed to take clear-cut actions to help the family get back on the right track.

Many parents, like Fred and Marge, find that their children are becoming prodigals right under their noses. Maybe you are feeling that way right now. Before I give you some suggestions for recognizing the beginning signs of a prodigal attitude, let me caution you about labeling.

BEWARE OF FALSE LABELING

We are often tempted to label our children. We sometimes think, for example, *All young people with long hair, mod clothes, and a disheveled appearance are probably druggies*. Parents sometimes find it easier to label their child as a "prodigal" or a "bad kid" than to effectively minister to the child's needs and accept responsibility for failing in some roles as parents.

Other times, parents label children as prodigals because they do not understand the normal process of growing up and becoming a self-sufficient adult. They forget that this process requires children to question, challenge, explore, and decide for themselves. We must be careful not to label our child as a "prodigal" if he or she chooses a slightly different way of life from our own. If a child is raised in a Bible-believing Baptist home and decides to become a member of a Bible-believing Presbyterian or Pentecostal church after he attends college, the parents should not think of him as a prodigal. Though the child has changed some of his beliefs, he is still professing Christ and His values.

Different Christian denominations also have differing man-made taboos. Some groups firmly believe that a woman should not wear pants or make-up if she is godly, yet others see nothing wrong with this. In some Christian groups dancing is considered a sin, but dancing is not associated with sin in other churches.

Sometimes our denominational and cultural ties are

stronger than our understanding of the body of Christ and the application of the gospel in various cultures. We must always ask ourselves if our children have forsaken Christ or merely our traditions. (I have in mind traditions not based on clear biblical teaching.) If only our traditions have been forsaken, then we need to rejoice in our children's Christian faith and seek to broaden our own perceptions of the Kingdom of God.

Finally, let's consider the thorny area of politics. Many parents hold strong views concerning political philosophies. We may raise our children to think that one particular political position more completely reflects the Christian world view. Yet, as the young person begins to think about political matters, he may come to a different conclusion. We must understand that as long as our children truly believe that their political position is consistent with the gospel message, we cannot label them as prodigals. Sincere Christians disagree on political issues, and our children deserve the same liberty to think for themselves.

Ask yourself if you are making one of these mistakes. If so, your child may not be adopting a prodigal attitude, and you should resist suggesting the child is a "bad kid." Often teens unconsciously accept your judgment, and the prophecy becomes self-fulfilling.

If you are not making one of these mistakes, then your child's actions might reflect a prodigal attitude. Many parents ask me, "How can I recognize the beginning of the prodigal process so that I can respond to it with effective measures?"

I tell them to evaluate the child's four basic relationships: God, family, the environment and self. The prodigal process begins when our child fails to allow the dynamic principles revealed in the Bible to control these relationships.

PRINCIPLES FOR DETECTING
A PRODIGAL ATTITUDE

Although analyzing these relationships can be helpful in detecting the first signs of a prodigal attitude, these signs can be symptoms of a number of other problems as well. Judging your child's actions in these areas must be done with great caution and love.

I will begin by suggesting the ideal relationship in each of these areas. Since no one is perfect, this ideal will rarely be achieved. Then I will repeat some of the comments parents have made to me, which suggest either normal or prodigal behavior in their children. Consider your own child as you read through these comments. (Throughout this discussion I will vary the sex of the child to avoid the use of the awkward he or she designation.)

Relationship with God

Ideal

A personal commitment to the person of Jesus Christ as Savior is evident in the child's life. The child has a sincere and thoughtful acceptance of the biblical faith and demonstrates this by a consistent application of the Christian faith to all areas of life. He or she joyfully participates in private and public worship.

Obviously many adults have trouble consistently applying the Christian faith to all areas of their lives, so this ideal is a goal parents set for their children, not something they expect the children to attain.

Normal

1. "Debbie wants to visit other churches. She often complains about our church and says she is bored with the services."

This child lives an outwardly moral life and has made some type of profession of faith in Christ. Yet, for the most part, she is a nominal Christian, lacking real spiritual zeal. She demonstrates no consistent love for God the Father or commitment to Jesus Christ. At times she will sincerely search for a better experience and knowledge of God and Christ.

2. "Mike asks me, 'Do you really believe in God? How do you know He exists?' I'm not sure that he really is searching for truth as much as trying to make fun of our beliefs."

Sometimes teens doubt their faith, even as some adults do, and they may seem to be ridiculing parents' beliefs rather than seriously searching for the truth. Often a child is only parroting the questions and reflecting the antagonism he gets from his peers. He may not feel he has adequate answers himself, so he is trying to see if his parents do. The normal child will eventually begin to resolve these questions if parents take time to answer him seriously.

Beginning Prodigal

1. "My daughter and her friends are experimenting with Ouija boards and tarot cards at slumber parties. Should I be concerned about this?"

Sometimes teens begin to study non-Christian religions seriously—the cults and the occult. This may imply a total rejection of the Christian religion or the acceptance of ideas that are humanistic, hedonistic, or secular. They may play with astrology, Ouija boards, tarot cards, and games like Dungeons and Dragons that promote occult practices.

At this stage the teen is testing a hodgepodge of differing ideas and still occasionally speaks about God and Christ. However, there is a tendency for this child to begin to forsake the ethical teachings and practices of the Christian faith. Parents need to tell their children that Ouija boards, tarot cards, and other games are not harmless toys but part of the paraphernalia of the occult, which Christians believe is empowered by satanic forces opposed to the God of the universe.

2. "Every Sunday morning at our house we argue about whether or not my son is going to church. My answer is always the same, but the arguments continue Sunday after Sunday. Each time he seems more rebellious and defiant."

Arguments about the necessity of attending church or about religious beliefs and ethical values become very heated at this stage. This shows that the child is not just testing an idea but beginning to accept another lifestyle.

Prodigal

1. "My son has become a Moonie." Or: "My son told me that the Bible is filled with lies and that we all evolved by chance and were not created."

The prodigal child finally accepts a non-Christian religion, cult, or secular philosophy of life. He may be merely adopting the current idea of the me-generation, a purely selfish and secular view of life. The child may still acknowledge the existence of some vague form of God. But at this stage, there is usually open hostility or cold indifference to the Christian beliefs of the parents.

Relationships with Others

Ideal

Parents. The child respects and loves his parents and seeks their counsel and advice. He or she is able to communicate openly and honestly with them about ideas and feelings and can listen to their feedback.

Siblings. The child loves his or her brothers and sisters and is not overly jealous or competitive with any of the siblings. When arguments do occur between this child and a brother or sister, he or she is able to admit his or her faults or forgive the sibling so that reconciliation occurs.

Peers. The child chooses friends who are responsible and stable and is able to socialize with others without compromising his or her own ethical standards. This child has an intrinsic commitment to avoid compromising situations and sexual sin. When sexual purity is tarnished in any manner, whether mentally or physically, he or she is able to apply God's grace in Jesus through repentance.

Normal

1. "I know Claudia loves and respects us, but she seems unable to share her deepest feelings with us."

At times all teens find it hard to seek their parents' counsel and advice because they fear rejection or negative feedback. *If I tell them too much,* the teen thinks, *they may not let me go to my friends' parties again.* If the atmosphere in the home encourages open and honest communication, a significant change from straightforward communication to an atmosphere of awkward silence or verbal confrontation will easily be detected.

2. "Charles says that we favor his younger brother. We really try to be fair, but Teddy is much more willing to accept our guidelines, so we don't fight with him as much."

Most children sometimes feel as if they are the stepchild of the family. Competition between siblings for the parents' attention and love is normal. However, the average child will resolve disagreements with the siblings and still enjoy being with them.

3. "Jean is very social and likes to be popular with the kids at school. Sometimes I wonder if she compromises her Christian values."

Most teens need to be accepted by their peer group; yet, they may not be abandoning an outwardly moral lifestyle. Instead, they may be attempting to appear and sound more worldly than they really are. Under sufficient social pressure, teens will sometimes compromise personal ethical standards and smoke cigarettes or drink alcohol in order to maintain their friendships. Their actions are often followed by feelings of remorse, self-incrimination, and depression.

The child confused by the conflicting ethics of her peers, her own emotions, and the moral teaching of the family, is often motivated to do well in school, but not so well that she hurts her relationships with her friends by looking too bright.

Questions about sex usually focus more on, How far can I go without sinning? than on the desire to be sexually pure. As the prodigal repeatedly takes her behavior to the very brink of what she considers wrong, she may falter and go beyond what she intended. If the deep guilt and depression that results is not effectively dealt with by her claiming the forgiveness of Christ and deciding on a pure lifestyle, the child often lives with a guilty conscience for years. Guilt, then, and not Christ's command, motivates her to remain outwardly pure.

A dangerous cycle can begin if the child thinks her purity has been lost. She begins to lower her standards and becomes more likely to have a so-called sexual accident while dating. This usually leads to more guilt, the acceptance of a lower view of herself, and the increased probability of sexual sin. However, if the child does not plan to engage in sex on a regular basis and still wants to maintain Christian standards, her guilt and frustration may finally motivate her to search for a more dynamic spiritual life.

Beginning Prodigal

1. "Any time we disagree with David, he refuses to listen to our reasons. Instead he shuts himself in his room. In fact, he rarely spends any time with the family anymore."

A radical change in a child's behavior, which eliminates interaction with the family, may be a sign of a prodigal attitude. Often the child will isolate himself in his room or refuse to participate in family activities. Teenagers are normally busy with friends and activities, but these activities may seem to be designed to avoid fellowship with other family members, especially parents.

The minute Tammy Sutton and her father reached home after Tammy had been suspended from school, she retreated to her room and immediately fell asleep. Fred knew she was probably sleeping off the alcohol. But he realized, then, that Tammy rarely spent time with Marge and him, and her brother, Luke, didn't seem to be around much either.

At dinner that night Tammy seemed repentant about her behavior: "I'm really sorry for putting you out like this. Suzanne and I just had the bad luck to get caught.

"A lot of kids drink, and it was our very first time," she assured her parents. "Don't worry. It will never happen again."

Fred and Marge doubted that this incident was really the first time Tammy had experimented with liquor. They talked for hours that evening and each night the rest of the week attempting to decide just what they should do. Then they consulted several Christian counselors and their pastors, who told them their suspicion was probably well-founded—lying to parents is often part of prodigal behavior.

Prodigal children are purposely deceptive, and, in fact, have a hidden life parents know nothing about. Parents may find that their child has been skipping school, lying about where he or she has been, or sneaking out at night.

Only two weeks after Tammy was suspended, the Sutton family was awakened one morning at three o'clock by a policeman who had their son, Luke, at his side. "I found Luke and two other boys walking around the neighborhood," he explained.

Fred thanked the policeman, pulled Luke into the house, and waited for the officer to walk to his car. Then, in a voice trembling with anger, he asked, "What were you boys doing out at this time? What are you trying to do, scare us half to death?"

Luke shrugged his shoulders and mumbled, "Sorry, we just wanted to go out to get something to eat." He retreated to his bedroom without giving any other reason.

Tammy had half a smile on her face until her father's stare reminded her of her own unacceptable behavior.

Fred and Marge were unable to sleep for the rest of the night, fearful that Luke would sneak out again and not return. Now the Suttons realized that they had two children becoming prodigals.

2. "Gene seems to lie to us all the time anymore. He even lies to his brothers and makes up the craziest excuses to get out of spending time with the family."

The beginning prodigal uses excuses (or outright lies) to avoid family activities, and the company of peers is always preferred over interaction with family members. He develops a "friend versus parents" mentality and frequently throws accusations at the parents. "You are just too old-fashioned." "You don't really love me, or you'd understand me as my friends do." Arguments become more and more frequent and center around the prodigal's breaking curfews, leaving chores undone, falling grades, breaking school rules, choosing the wrong friends, and skipping school. Frequent drinking in social situations may occur at this stage as well as the use of illegal drugs.

Since most parents encourage the attainment of good grades in school, children harboring prodigal attitudes may purposely reject academic achievement as a worthwhile value. They literally sabotage their own grades, as Tammy Sutton did. This prodigal behavior is seen most clearly when children have always attained good grades. However, we must be very careful to be sure that no other factors are disturbing the child.

3. "Allison never sees her junior-high friends any-

more. Instead she seems to be associating with kids whose values seem quite different from ours."

Teens who are becoming prodigals often reject their Christian friends (either because the Christian friends reject the teen's current behavior or because the Christian friends now seem boring). Beginning prodigals then begin to associate with new friends who have a wild lifestyle.

Always allow for the "odd couple" situation, however. Your child may befriend a teen with different values to help him or her. You need to be concerned about such a situation, though, and recognize that only an exceptional young person can resist the temptation to conform to the beliefs, values, and actions of his or her friends.

Many times a child who is becoming a prodigal tries to replace the intimacy of the family with the intimacy of romance. The child willingly surrenders to the sexual drive and rarely feels remorse. Such acts are justified as an emotional release from the strains of an unhappy, lonely life. When found without an excuse or a believable lie to cover up his unacceptable behavior, the child usually places the blame on someone else—parents, society, school—rather than accept personal responsibility. "No one cares for or loves me, so how do you expect me to act?" the child protests.

Prodigal

1. "John comes and goes as he pleases. Sometimes he disappears for days at a time, and he never tells us where he's been."

The prodigal child now openly rejects parental and school authority. "I will do what I want, when I want to do it," the child asserts. Even in public, the teen is defiant and disrespectful, though he or she may still secretly respect and love the parents.

This is actually what happened at the Sutton's house. The day after the policeman brought Luke home, he announced that he was no longer going to attend private school. "I want to transfer to public school," he said, adding, "If you won't transfer me, I'll just skip school and flunk out."

Although the prodigal may maintain close ties with some brothers and sisters in order to gain emotional support and approval from them, he or she only stays at home to eat, sleep, and argue. Teens may eventually run away, and adult prodigals, if they are financially independent, will usually break ties with their parents in a moment of anger. In extreme cases, the young adult may physically attack one of the parents during a confrontation.

Relationship to the Environment

Ideal

The child has a good sense of sharing and feels comfortable in the physical environment of the home and school. While she enjoys the privacy of her own room, she is not threatened when other members of the family visit her. She cares for the appearance of her room and her clothes. She also respects others' property and space.

Normal

1. "I can never get Heidi to clean her room. She leaves her clothes lying on the floor, right where she took them off. She never makes her bed. When I

complain about this, she acts as if I'm asking too much of her. 'You're always nagging me,' she says."

The normal child will at times demonstrate a selfish and irresponsible attitude. She may feel uncomfortable sharing a room with a sibling and fail to take proper care of her personal property. Generally, she may not mind others coming into her room, but at times she will become overly concerned about her privacy.

Beginning Prodigal

1. "David does not want anyone in his room, even his younger brother, who used to be close to him."

When a child's main concern is to define what rooms in the house, physical objects, segments of time and money, belong exclusively to him, this can be a warning that he is rejecting the values and beliefs of the home and developing a prodigal attitude. The beginning prodigal may also have a careless attitude towards the property of others or the physical appearance of the home. However, this may also be the teen's normal desire to express individuality and self-sufficiency, so be careful not to use this as your only indication of a problem.

Prodigal

1. "Megan frequently locks her bedroom door. No one is allowed inside, even to clean. In fact, we never see her anymore. She's either in her room or gone."

The prodigal may attempt to act as if she were living in a separate apartment. She may avoid being in the areas of the house where interaction with other family members is possible. She is never home for meals and often not even in the house until after the parents' usual bedtime. In extreme cases, the child may physically damage the parents' property.

Relationship with Self

Ideal

The child realizes that he is made in the image of God and has been given unique abilities by Him. While he rejoices in what God has given him, he accepts his limitations and failures, knowing that he is a sinner without virtue outside of God's redeeming grace. The child tries to grow in faith and love and is at peace with God's plan for his life. Although he experiences hurts, turmoil, pain, and disappointment, this child works through these feelings from the perspective of his Christian faith and is willing to seek help from others.

Normal

1. "Matt knows that he is loved by God, yet he still feels inadequate and inferior at times. Sometimes I worry when he seems particularly despondent or upset."

Even though a child has claimed Christ as Savior, he may still be confused about how God is able to continually forgive him for his sins. Sometimes he will be depressed or feel guilty about his sin. Therefore, he will either attempt to rationalize his behavior so he can think better of himself or live in a melancholy state, wondering if he is worth anything at all.

At times he may feverishly try to improve his attitude, focusing on a certain talent to make himself feel special. If he fails in this area he may become depressed; if he succeeds, he may become overly proud.

Beginning Prodigal

1. "Ben spends much of his time sleeping. I know something is wrong because he always seems half asleep—or drugged—but he won't talk to me or to a counselor about what's wrong."

A young adult who is becoming a prodigal sees himself as being alone and having to depend upon himself for success and gratification. He still struggles with the questions of right and wrong, so he frequently feels angry, frustrated, and unfulfilled. To resolve his anxiety, he uses drugs or alcohol or sexual encounters to give him pleasure and release from the tension. Excessive amounts of sleep help him escape from reality. He doubts that he is loved by God and lacks the faith and trust to seek help from others. Tammy Sutton's use of alcohol seems to have been the means by which she attempted to deal with her feelings of frustration and boredom. As time went on, her parents discovered that Tammy would frequently become drunk and would even drink alone in her room.

Prodigal

1. "Sherry is constantly high on drugs. She never seems to care anymore about her appearance or about anything except pot."

This prodigal teen has either decided that she is worthless or has become so self-assured about her rejection of Christianity that she does not care how she acts. She purposely ignores the deeper questions raised by her outright rejection of Christian moral values. Her regular abuse of drugs and alcohol and sexual promiscuity assure her that her rejection of Christian values will lead to pleasure, not to pain. She may be physically violent toward her parents so she can reinforce her necessary feeling of superiority.

2. "Howard is popular and confident and he is the quarterback of the football team. I am so proud of him. Yet, he is so distant from us and rarely talks. He told me the other day that he believed in himself and that was the only way to make it in life."

Sometimes the prodigal process stems from an individual's accepting a sophisticated, "me-first" attitude toward life, which leaves no room for prayer, God, or Christianity. Such a person may be successful and ruthless in attaining success. Clashes occur in the family because the young person feels his parents' faith is useless and outdated. He withdraws from the family except for times when they can be used to help him obtain his own goals. This prodigal is simply looking out for "number one," solely motivated to accomplish things for his own pleasure.

In the natural maturing process, a child will have some conflicts with parents. However, when the process begins to tear down the fundamental relationships within the family—a common faith in God, a shared ethical standard, respect of and love for parents, and a sense of community—the prodigal process has begun.

A FINAL WORD OF WARNING

A final word of warning needs to be added here. We must assess whether or not the trouble we are having with our children is a personality conflict or his or her outright rebellion against our beliefs and ethical standards. Many times parents mistake a conflict of personalities for a rebellious child.

You may be very athletic, yet your son may prefer reading books to playing baseball or basketball. He may only have a few close friends and avoid social events, whereas you are socially minded. If you are not careful, you may try to push your son into your personality mold and accuse him of being rebellious if he resists. Unfortunately, all of us have difficulty accepting others for who they are, especially our children.

The apostle Paul's simile of the necessity of each part of the body (with dissimilar functions) for the health of the entire body is as applicable to the family as it is to the church. Our children may have interests and abilities that keep them from fulfilling our dreams for them, but by developing these abilities, they are fulfilling God's will for their lives. We should not allow these differences to cause division in our homes.

HOW TO HANDLE THE EARLY SIGNS OF A PRODIGAL ATTITUDE

Once you recognize the signs that the prodigal process has begun, the first rule is DO NOT PANIC! If your heart is filled with outrage, frustration, and anger, you have already reacted out of panic and fear. Too many parents land squarely on top of their sons and daughters, giving them impassioned sermonettes that end with a barrage of actual or threatened punishments. Such outbursts usually increase a child's resentment and widen the communication gap between parents and children.

To avoid panicking, look to the future. What has been true in the past does not have to be true in the future. Changes can be made. You need to begin by reassessing your goals as parents.

THE BIBLICAL GOAL OF PARENTING

As parents see the prodigal process beginning, they must first clarify what they hope to accomplish as they raise this child. Sometimes it is wise for parents to enlist an extended family member or a friend to help them clarify this goal. Single parents might want to meet with a Christian counselor or pastor.

As you attempt to set a goal for Christian parenting, it is vital for you to reread Ephesians 6:1–4.

> Children, obey your parents in the Lord, for this is right. "Honor your father and mother," which is the first commandment with promise: "that it may be well with you and you may live long on the earth." And you, fathers, do not provoke your children to wrath, but bring them up in the training and admonition of the Lord.

Our goal as Christian parents should be to bring our children up "in the training and admonition of the Lord," as this passage of Scripture suggests. The Greek word for *training* is *paideia*, which means to provide instructive experiences in order to educate a child. *Training* means being a positive role model, thereby showing our children how to live and providing verbal correction when they fail to follow us in what is right. It also includes, when these approaches fail, the stronger measures of chastisement.

The second word that defines the goal of parenting is *admonition,* which in the Greek text is the word *nouthesia.* This word is derived from two words: *nous,* which means mind, and *titheme,* which means to put or to place. The word *admonition* literally means "to put or place something in the mind." This instruction begins with a clear warning that fathers are not to provoke their children to anger. This instruction should obviously be done in an attitude of gentleness, taking care to cause no harm. A harsh, unloving, or "don't ask-questions-just-believe" type of instruction in Christian doctrine does not fit the Greek word *nouthesia*.

In this passage of Scripture parents are commanded to provide encouragement, a positive example, realistic goals, sensitivity, advice, reproof, and remonstration for their children. To be effective parents, we must strive to have all these dimensions.

The need for such a balanced approach is pointed out by Donald Sloat in his book *The Dangers of Growing Up in a Christian Home*. He states:

> Several problems, or danger points, can occur as we attempt to pass our values to our children. First, parents (and the church as well) may instill so much fear and guilt along with values that youngsters are afraid to sort out their beliefs in order to stand on their own. This is what happened to me as I grew up, and I believe it is common in the evangelical church. A second problem exists when youngsters accept what their parents have taught them without questioning or evaluating it. They are then simply following hollow beliefs that can crumble easily under pressure. This is especially true when Christian parents either do not teach children to think for themselves, or do not even allow them to do so.[2]

Because of these two problems it is vital that we develop an atmosphere where our children are encouraged to know not only what we believe but also why we believe it. Parents must allow their children to work through questions of truth and ethics, even as we attempt to influence them with the message and standards of Christ. Only as our children become convinced that the Christian faith and values are true will they become committed to these beliefs that will hold up for a lifetime.

Parents' failure to understand this necessity may explain why many "Christian kids" lose their faith and morals when they go to college. Once away from home, the children are free to go through this natural process of becoming their own person without pressure from their parents to conform. However, in the environment of most colleges, people going through this maturing process have a tendency to allow their behavior and beliefs to go to extremes, jumping wholeheartedly into non-Christian religions, worldly philosophies, cults, and "partying"—that is, sexual promiscuity and drug and alcohol abuse.

We also must understand that creating such an atmosphere in our homes will mean allowing our children to differ with us on minor theological points, such as the meaning of the sacraments, worship styles, the charismatic gifts, and the role of women in the church. Not all Christians agree on these and other matters; yet, this does not make them any less Christian. Our main concern should be for our children to share our convictions concerning what C. S. Lewis called "mere Christianity" and not every jot and tittle of doctrine of our particular denomination. Making a major issue of a minor point will only alienate us from our children and perhaps discourage them from holding to the vital areas of Christian dogma.

Now that you understand your child's actions better and have assessed your parenting goals, we will consider a biblical parenting strategy. In the next chapter, we will be talking about this strategy in relation to the prodigal child, but this parenting approach is valid for every child.

5

Can a Prodigal Remain at Home?

A modern proverb states, "If we fail to plan, we plan to fail." There's a lot of truth in that. Parents who realize that their children are becoming prodigals need to develop a positive parenting strategy which will effectively reach their children with the love and grace of Christ.

Although each parenting strategy must be unique—custom tailored to the needs, circumstances, and personality of the child God has given us—the Bible does help us establish a framework that can be used to develop our particular strategy. This framework is based on the relationship God has with His children, which is seen in His actions towards His people. Since God is our perfect, divine parent, we should model our actions after Him. He has always related to men through the covenant relationship.

THE COVENANT RELATIONSHIP

Dr. Jack and Judith Balswick, who teach sociology, family development, and family therapy at Fuller Theological Seminary, have applied God's covenant concept to parenting.[1] They set forth the idea that God's relationship with His people is always within the context of this covenant, so our role as parents should also be kept within the framework of a covenant relationship with our children.

I believe this covenant relationship has four dimensions: unconditional love and grace, authority, the law, and intimacy. Let's look at each one and as we do so, develop a biblical parenting strategy. Within these four dimensions of the covenantal parenting strategy I will suggest seven practical steps. These steps are not listed in the order that parents may want to apply them but under the appropriate dimension of the covenant relationship.

FIRST DIMENSION: UNCONDITIONAL LOVE

Unconditional love is at the center of God's covenant with His people. Briefly summarized, the covenant began when God chose to be in a relationship of love with Abraham and revealed Himself to him. Abraham did not earn this revelation by being good or because he was any less involved in idol worship than others in Ur of Chaldees. Rather, God in His grace chose to be intimate with Abraham and work His redemption through him. (See Gen. 12.)

God promised that He would bless the seed of Abraham and bring salvation to all nations through Him. Abraham's true descendants would ultimately be revealed as those people who had the same faith in God's promise of a Messiah as Abraham had in God's promise to Him (Rom. 4). God in unconditional love reaches out to His people. We do not choose Him, but He chooses us.

The covenant, though based on God's unconditional love, was intended to be a reciprocal agreement. God would care for His people by revealing Himself to them, working wonders in their midst, delivering them from danger, forgiving their sins, providing temporal needs, giving them victory over their enemies, and pouring out His Spirit upon them. His Spirit would strengthen them to live in this fallen world. In response His covenant people would care about Him and desire to obey His law.

Did the Hebrew people appreciate these gifts enough to

79

walk in faith and keep the commandments of God? In most circumstances they failed to respond to God's love as they should have. Look at the list of their kings who broke the first Commandment by practicing idolatry or allowing their subjects to do so: Rehoboam, Ahaziah, Joash, Amaziah, Ahaz, Manasseh, and Amon. (And the Israelites were only ruled by kings for 433 years.) The Hebrew people were prodigals. Yet God still loved them unconditionally, sending messages of love, reconciliation, rebuke, warning, and discipline to them through His prophets.

God's unconditional love for us is the central theme of the parable of the prodigal son. Just look at how the father responded to the son's request for his inheritance, which he had no right to claim until his father's death. The father granted this unusual favor.

Any Jew who heard Jesus tell this parable would have known the Old Testament law which prescribed how a father should respond to rebellious behavior. The same chapter in Deuteronomy that contains the law concerning inheritance also declares that an ungodly adult son who devoted himself to a godless, hedonistic lifestyle is to be given the death penalty:

> If a man has a stubborn and rebellious son who will not obey the voice of his father or the voice of his mother, and who, when they have chastened him, will not heed them, then his father and his mother shall take hold of him and bring him out to the elders of his city, to the gate of his city. And they shall say to the elders of his city, "This son of ours is stubborn and rebellious; he will not obey our voice; he is a glutton and a drunkard."
>
> Then all the men of his city shall stone him to death with stones; so you shall put away the evil person from among you, and all Israel shall hear and fear.
>
> Deuteronomy 21:18–21

The father of the prodigal son could have accused his son of being a profligate. The father could have thrown the first stone since the law says, "all the men" shall stone him, and watched his son bleed to death from the gaping wounds. Instead, this father gave the son his full inheritance. Talk about unconditional love!

The parable points out that as prodigal children we deserve death, yet God has given us an inheritance of grace which allows us to live and have time to repent. The heavenly Father has not given his prodigals what they deserve, but He has poured upon them mercy rather than justice.

Parents must recognize that their relationship with their child is also based on unconditional love. The child is born into our care by God's providence and we must decide to love this bundle of unrestrained emotion and desires called a baby. We choose to love this child unconditionally just as God loves us.

Parents must decide to continue to offer this child unconditional love throughout his life. This is an action, a decision, an attitude of heart, that must be based on God's love for us and renewed each day of our lives, regardless of what our children have done to us. Our relationship with our children is not based on their actions, but on God's unconditional love, which we share with our children.

Yet God's covenant of unconditional love goes beyond the one-way relationship. This love hopes for a bilateral relationship in which the child responds with love. God loves us and desires us to love Him. We love our children and hope that they will love us. However, if the child's love for us is weakened or gone altogether, we never abandon our part of the covenant, just as God continues to love His people even during times of rebellion.

Unconditional love is very different from two popular

relationships today: the open relationship in which people choose to stay together only as long as they continue to meet each other's needs and the contract relationship in which a legal document assures the fair protection of everyone's rights and names each person's responsibilities.

The first relationship, the open relationship, is common in many marriages today, and is unfortunately becoming the basis for many parent/child relationships. If a spouse or a child fails to provide positive input, the relationship can be terminated. Commitment and sacrificial, unilateral love are unheard of in this relationship.

The contract relationship is more closely akin to God's covenant with his people. Most of God's promises involve a responsibility on the part of the person who receives the blessing. For instance, when God established the covenant between Himself and Abraham He declared ". . . Abraham shall surely become a great and mighty nation, and all the nations of the earth shall be blessed in him. For I have known him, in order that he may command his children and his household after him, that they keep the way of the LORD, to do righteousness and justice, that the LORD may bring to Abraham what He has spoken to him" (Gen. 18:18–19).

Yet the relationship between God and His people still involves unconditional love. Although His people may not receive the blessings of the covenant if they do not follow His ways, God will still love and work with them. It is for this reason that the contract approach cannot stand alone as these marriage contracts do. This type of relationship must be immersed in the larger framework of covenant love and commitment or it will breed a harsh moralism, legalism, and self-righteousness.

A pure contract relationship would allow parents to see their children as being beyond redemption, as the Pharisees saw the prostitutes and sinners of their times. That's why they cut them off from their love, mercy, and grace. Yet Christianity is distinguished from all other religions because of its teaching that people are saved and redeemed totally on the basis of God's love and grace provided in Jesus Christ and not on their own efforts. Just as God was willing to be patient and work with the Hebrew people because of His covenant with Abraham, so we, too, must be willing to be patient with our children and show them understanding and grace.

Parents must develop a parenting strategy that is based on the solid foundation of unconditional love. How can we do this? Begin by praying together for your child.

Step One: Establish the consistent practice of praying with fervent and honest intensity on behalf of your child.

You would be surprised at the number of times parents face a crisis without any time specifically set aside for praying for the wayward child. Prayer is, in some ways, the easiest responsibility we have. Yet many of us resist prayer since it calls us to recognize that we are not sufficient to meet the needs of our child without divine help. It is humbling and somewhat frightening to recognize that we need God to act in our child's heart for any of our efforts to have a permanent effect.

Fred and Marge Sutton had difficulty with this first step in developing a covenant relationship with their children. They had never prayed or studied the Bible together so this felt awkward to them. Both were "self-made" professionals, and although they prayed occasionally, they had never experienced a deep prayer life. Both of them had to seek help from their pastor, and even after that, prayer was still an area of weakness for them as it is for many of us.

Yet from the divine viewpoint prayer is without doubt the most important step in this process. Prayer allows us to express all four of the dimensions of the covenant with God. As we pray, we depend on God's *unconditional love* and *grace* found in Jesus Christ. We bow to His *authority* and knowledge and are confident that He is able to lead us and our children to a mature faith. We acknowledge our responsibility to obey His *law*, and we demonstrate our desire to have *intimacy* in our relationship with Him.

While many of us may not have been conscious of these four dimensions as we prayed, they are part of the intimate relationship of prayer. Prayer can help them become a part of our family life, and it is an essential part of any biblical parenting strategy.

DIMENSION TWO: AUTHORITY

God claims absolute authority, kingship, and power over his people. Yet He uses this position to serve His children, to bring them to maturity, and to empower them to live truly abundant lives. God is not a divine despot or a cruel dictator. As revealed in Jesus Christ, God is clearly the "Servant King."

One of the last things Jesus did before He died was to model the servant relationship. He washed His disciples feet during the Last Supper. We instinctively know what a sacrifice this was, since the foot is the dirtiest, smelliest part of the body. Yet, in the Jewish culture this task was considered so humbling that even a slave could not be commanded to do it. Only disciples who wanted to express their loving devotion to a rabbi would perform this service voluntarily.

Christ, the teacher and leader of this group, not the student, purposely took off his loose, upper garments to assume the simple garb of a servant. He washed each of the disciples' feet, and then purposely told them the meaning of this action. "If I then, your Lord and Teacher, have washed your feet, you also ought to wash one another's feet" (John 13:14). Jesus used this graphic illustration to show the future leaders of His church that God does not want those in authority to be abusive or overbearing, but rather to use their position to serve those under them.

Authority in the Family

God, the Father, is the ruler of His people, and the human father is head of his family. Both parents have authority over their children. The parenting relationship with the child is a lifetime endeavor, ever growing in its depth, beauty, and complexity. Throughout this relationship the parents should use their God-ordained leadership position not to oppress their children, but rather to serve them with the intention of empowering them to be able to live a life pleasing to God, beneficial to others, and filled with divine peace.

Indeed as our children grow older and begin to walk in the faith, the empowering process begins to flow both ways and the family becomes even richer and stronger as they also learn how to serve us and encourage our faith.

The next steps in a biblical parenting strategy suggest ways to use your leadership to change the direction of the beginning prodigal child's thinking.

Step Two: Parents need to suggest some positive activities outside of the sphere of the family which will allow the prodigal to develop a responsible nature.

Parents may be shocked to find out that the laws of God's creation did not destine the time between puberty and adulthood to be one of frustration and conflict for both parents and children. It is important for us to realize that our society has created special tensions for adolescents, because of our technology, which demands advanced schooling. We are asking our young people, whose sexual desires awaken by the age of thirteen, to control their passions for at least five years. At the same time, we are not transferring the responsibilities of adulthood to our youth and, therefore, they have an unusual amount of free time.

This is diametrically opposed to the norms of most cultures during the last three thousand years according to Ronald L. Koteskey, who studied the history of adolescence in several civilizations.[2] In his studies he found that children were considered to be adults between the ages of twelve and fourteen in Hebrew, Roman, English, and American law. They were allowed to work for wages and to marry. This trend began to change in the 1850s, and eighteen only became the age of adulthood in the last century.

We need to resist our culture's trend to accept irresponsible actions from adolescents as the norm and to transfer responsibilities to our young people to help them grow into mature adults. Encouraging them to find a part-time job where possible would be a good idea, along with promoting the development of their own "home industries," such as babysitting or lawn mowing. For instance, the Suttons encouraged Tammy to take a job as a part-time secretary for a local church. She gained a sense of accomplishment from working and making her own money. The Suttons also found a job for Luke, but he quit after two weeks.

In light of this emphasis, we should also encourage our church youth groups to organize other activities than just social events. Young people could distribute leaflets that announce an evangelistic meeting, paint an older person's house, or volunteer to read to the blind or shut-ins. For instance, one Christian youth group from Dallas, Texas, travels to Chicago each summer to a program called "Summer in the City." These teens join teens from the Chicago suburbs to serve as playground supervisors in public housing units of the inner city and to help residents paint and restore rundown apartments.

In our own church here at Coral Ridge our teenagers are involved in summer missionary programs where they travel to foreign lands and help to build churches, hand out religious literature, plant fields, and distribute food. Such opportunities to share their faith and love have had profound effects on many of their lives.

Not only work but also sports, hobbies (some of which can be shared with parents, like needlepointing or woodworking), and lessons in piano, guitar, or other instruments encourage teens to develop their talent and learn useful skills.

In all of these ways parents can use their authority constructively to breed character in their young while striving to encourage them to be empowered to face the reality of life.

Step Three: Refer the child to other mature Christians who may be able to reach him or her.

The nuclear family of our culture needs to try to create an "extended family" of support people, much like the family in biblical times, which consisted of grandparents, cousins, and a vast host of relatives and paid servants. A covenant approach to parenting sees the family as part of a larger community of God's people. Parents need to recognize potential helpers within this family who are gifted in relating to young adults.

At times, parents should recommend that the child talk to a pastor or Christian counselor. Parents must admit that they are not able to answer many of the child's questions, and then entrust the child to a Christian worker who may be able to reach the child more effectively. Fred and Marge Sutton asked Tammy to go to a local alcohol abuse center. They demonstrated their love by actively participating in her counseling, supporting her efforts to overcome her drinking habit, and being patient when she faltered in her determination. Through this program Tammy was able to overcome her growing addiction. She was willing to accept responsibility for her mistakes and began to develop a good relationship with her parents. Again Luke resisted their efforts. He refused to seek counsel and became more and more distant.

THIRD DIMENSION: LAW

The relationship between God's grace and God's law is seldom understood. While sinful men cannot gain God's favor through obedience to His law, the Lord of the Covenant has given laws to His children for three reasons:

- So we will know the essential ethical principles that are necessary for a society
- So we will be aware of our need for God's grace and appreciate His love for us
- So we will have a loving guide to direct our lives

What practical value does this understanding of the law have for us as parents? First, it makes clear that unconditional love still expects obedience and responsibility from the person who is receiving this love.

Therefore, a family should establish laws that define each person's responsibilities within the family unit. Just rewards and punishments should be established for obeying or breaking these laws, just as God established blessings and curses for His covenant people (Deut. 28, Heb. 12). These rewards and penalties should be clearly understood by the entire family.

In such an atmosphere a child can break a rule, be punished, repent, receive forgiveness, and know that he is loved by his parents during the entire experience. Just as God's covenant of grace makes it possible for sinners to have a relationship with God, so the covenant in a family allows imperfect human beings to live together in a dynamic intercourse of love, responsibility, and forgiveness. This atmosphere of grace enables us to have a "loving contract" with our children, which avoids the dangers of legalism, moralism, and perfectionism.

The next step in establishing a covenant relationship with our children is to set up household rules or laws.

Step Four: Set up essential rules of the house so the adolescent prodigal can clearly see when she is openly rebelling.

Children must understand that as long as they are living at home, the parents will establish the standards of behavior. The list of rules should not be long and should only reflect minimally acceptable behavior, so that the atmosphere in the home can remain one of grace and growth. However, these rules must be comprehensive enough to cover all areas of this list.

1. Curfew

Parents need to set a time for children to be at home and in bed. Obviously this will be difficult if the parents stay up unusually late and do not live on a reasonable schedule themselves. Younger children must understand that older children can stay up later.

Children should also be responsible to let parents know where they are going and how they can be reached if an emergency occurs. Parents should also let someone know where they will be at all times.

2. Honesty

Since intimacy is the fourth dimension of the covenant, deception and hypocrisy will not be tolerated. To encourage honesty, you might consider making the punishment much less severe for a child who confesses his error before he gets caught. Again, the parents need to be honest with the children or the rule will be disregarded.

3. School Attendance

Skipping school is definitely outside the bounds of acceptable conduct. You might tell your children that you will be checking with the school on a regular basis to make sure everything is all right. At the same time you should become aware of the school's method of notifying parents when children are absent. Sometimes notification only occurs after extensive periods of truant behavior.

4. Behavior at School

Disobedience in school should result in punishment at home as well as at school, since parents expect their children to listen to teachers and school authorities, as the Bible suggests in 1 Peter 2:13. Remind the child that you will be in close contact with his teachers, so you will be aware of any misbehavior.

5. Required Chores

Each child should have responsibilities at home. Chores build a sense of responsibility, family pride, community spirit, and accomplishment. A loss of privileges and the giving of an allowance are a good punishment and reward for motivating children to accept responsibility.

6. Use of Drugs or Alcohol

Children need to understand that substance abuse only leads to unhappiness and destructive addiction. Parents must educate their children about the danger of alcohol and drug abuse by the time they are twelve, since drug use is becoming a problem for fourth through sixth grade students.

Parents need to make it clear to their children that they want them to be honest about any drug or alcohol problems they may face. They should know that any attempts to hide substance abuse or to reject counseling for such a problem will result in punishment.

7. Use of the Car

Only children who are sixteen and have a license can drive the family car. Parents who follow the speed limits and are not irresponsible in their own use of the car can establish the same rules for their children. Any irresponsible use of the vehicle will mean the loss of driving privileges for a predetermined period of time. In *Almost Thirteen*, author Claudia Arp, co-director of Marriage Alive Seminars and founder of Mom's Support Groups, suggests a driving contract between the parents and the teen which establishes rules and punishments. For instance: "Any speeding or parking tickets I get, I pay for myself."[3]

8. Dating Rules

You should establish definite "date nights" (Friday and Saturday) and talk to your child about the proper places teens should go on a date. Parents may want to require that the child's first dates take place at a family function or restrict dating to group affairs.

Again, education is an important part of these rules. In the early teens, or even by the age of twelve, our children need to receive godly instruction from us about sex. Parents should discuss proper sexual conduct and make sure their children understand both biological facts and Christian morals. We should promote an atmosphere of empathy and understanding and ask the child to confide in us if he or she faces difficult decisions.

9. Dress Code

Clothing is an important part of a young person's self-image and social acceptance. Specific rules which reflect the parent's taste rather than any ultimate standard should be avoided. A parent should mainly be concerned that a child's clothing is modest and does not suggest a promiscuous attitude.

10. Courtesy

Verbal abuse of other family members, even in a heated argument, must not be tolerated. Children need to understand that foul language destroys relationships and that they must try to learn to control their tempers.

These ten areas are only provided as general guidelines. Some homes may need more rules, others far fewer. The age of your children when you establish these rules also makes a difference as well as whether or not the prodigal process has begun. Parents who have prodigal children often limit their rules to the essentials—substance abuse, sex, hours, driving—because they recognize that the prodigal child has already rebelled against most of these rules. In such a case the parent should only attempt to set forth restrictions that protect the child from truly delinquent behavior.

Parents should plan to meet with the prodigal and the other children in the family privately. While parents need to work on the rules before they meet with the children, they need to allow the children to have input, too. Parents should be ready to answer a child's why-this-rule questions by explaining how the rule will benefit the child and the household. If the child has a valid reason to resist the rule, the parents should be flexible enough to adjust it.

Unreasonable rules contribute to children becoming prodigals.

The final list of rules could be reviewed by another Christian couple, pastor, or counselor to insure that there is no possible miscarriage of justice. Parents need to realize that some of their expectations may not be realistic and that conflict could develop because the standards do not fit the teen's level of development.

One single mother I counseled, Sarah, was having trouble with her daughter for this reason. She had set a curfew of sunset for Sue who was a teenager. That fall Sue missed her high school's football and basketball games, dances, and parties.

Sue went along with the rule until spring of that year. Then one night she sneaked out her bedroom window to go to a statewide track meet which was being held at the high school. Sarah caught her daughter sneaking back into the house at midnight.

She exploded with a barrage of accusations. "You little slut! You've been off messing around in the back seat with some boy I bet. I should have known you couldn't be trusted. How far did you go?"

Sue tried to explain. "No, Mom, it wasn't that way. I just wanted to go to the statewide track meet. I have never parked with a boy. Please believe me."

Sarah finally controlled her temper when she saw the tears in Sue's eyes. Sarah had no proof of her accusations. She had just presupposed that her daughter would get into trouble if she was out after dark. Sarah tried to tell Sue she was sorry, but Sue ran to her bedroom.

As Sarah lay awake that night listening to Sue crying in the other room, she decided to seek Christian counseling. This led her to reevaluate the rules in their household.

Sarah's mistake may be obvious to many of us, yet we need to be careful or we will do the same thing. The rules we set should reflect a positive, yet realistic, evaluation of our child's character. Children must also understand, however, that the home is not a democracy. The authority of the parents is the second dimension of the covenant relationship and is brought to bear upon the home through the third dimension of law. Our parenting strategy must be firmly fixed upon these two covenant realities and we must structure our family in this manner to be truly effective parents.

Once the final set of rules has been established, the family should have a meeting, perhaps informally after dinner, to announce the rules and to talk about rewards for keeping them and punishments for breaking them.

Individual and family rewards are an important part of the biblical relationship since a blessing, rather than a curse, always accompanies obedience to God's law and is the real hope of parents. One way to bring the idea of blessing into your family may be, if all your children keep the rules well for a month, to have a special outing which the children will enjoy. If one child breaks a few rules in a month and then improves the next month, the parents might give that child a special privilege.

It is also important that the punishment "fit the crime." For instance, breaking curfew rules could "ground" the teen, restricting her right to leave the house for a few days. Or the use of alcohol might eliminate his car privileges for a month.

For rules to be effective, the penalty must be enforceable by the parents. As you develop your strategy, you need to make a list of penalties that are clearly under your control. For example, withdrawal of an allowance is effective only if the child does not have a separate source of income from cutting yards or a part-time job. However, if the child needs the parents' permission to have a part-time job, and he has been abusing the right to work by going out with friends afterwards without telling the parents, then the parents can revoke their permission for the child to work.

You should also be sure that you are willing to consistently enforce the punishment. If a child is not allowed to stay overnight at a friend's house for a month, you must be willing to enforce this punishment even if you want to go away for a weekend. (Either cancel your plans or hire an adult sitter.)

After the rules have been discussed and finalized the parents could close the meeting by leading their children in prayer dedicating their family to the care and love of God. They should pray that the behavior of all members of the family—parents, too—would be pleasing to Him.

Limits of the Covenant

God's covenant does have limits. While God's people do not have to be perfect in order to remain in the covenant, they do need to respond to God's unconditional love with some degree of faith, repentance, and love. Unconditional love is not love without a backbone, nor is it a doormat love. The dimension of law within the covenant makes this plain.

A total, persistent and stubborn unbelief and rejection of God, His laws, and His love cuts us off from the Lord of the Covenant. This separation, the most severe chastisement of all, only comes after His patience has been met with hypocrisy, rebellion, and continual sin.

Yes, the Israelites were loved by God when they disobeyed. But they were also punished for their sins. Their continual rebellion against God's love resulted in seventy years of captivity in Babylon. Later, when they rejected Jesus as their Messiah, God punished them by destroying Jerusalem.

In a similar manner, God told Israel to "cut off" those

who openly rebelled against Him and His laws. He even instructed parents whose children utterly rejected His ways to turn them over to the state for punishment. God also commands His modern-day church to excommunicate those who live in continual and unrepentant sin.

Why? God hopes that excommunication will cause the person to repent, and He wishes to protect others in the church from the influence of this sin. These examples show us that God does not allow His grace to be abused where He is mocked or manipulated (Gal. 6:7). Also, the most loving act is to let people see where their sin is taking them.

In establishing rules for the home, parents must clearly state that although the prodigal is loved, continual rebellion will result in removal from the house. It is not loving to give our children the impression that unrepented sin does not have consequences.

As you develop your strategy, write down the specific type of rebellion that would cause you to ask the child to leave. Then communicate these guidelines to the child in a loving way. You must also decide where the child will be sent if removal becomes necessary. To a private school? To a drug rehabilitation center? To a member of the extended family who has experience in working with young adults? To a home for delinquent children?

Teenage prodigals are not the only prodigals who may have to be kicked out of the house. Some parents find themselves in the position of Elaine, the widowed mother of Larry, a twenty-two year old who still lived with her and only worked sporadically. In order to have spending money, Larry took whatever was of value in the house and sold it. At one point Elaine was forced to place a padlock on her bedroom door to keep her personal belongings from being hocked. Obviously, Elaine should have told the young man to find his own apartment—and a job.

Most parents desire to avoid such drastic measures. However, sometimes such steps become necessary for the good of the child, the parents, other members of the family, and God's Kingdom. Grace and law must be maintained in a dynamic union. Together they form an indispensable part of your plan for dealing with your prodigal child from a biblical perspective.

FOURTH DIMENSION: INTIMACY

Eternal life, the ultimate benefit of the covenant, is described by Jesus as "knowing God the Father and His Son" (John 17:1–3). God desires to dwell with His people, and He expects a deep personal interaction to take place between Him and His children.

Only by constructing a framework of unconditional love, grace, law, and authority in our homes can we provide the foundation for intimacy with our children. This covenant allows understanding and security to exist within the parent/child relationship. Without this commitment, fear of rejection and alienation will keep our children from opening up to us.

The next steps in developing a covenant relationship will help you to establish intimacy.

Step Five: Dedicate specific times to spend with your child so you can establish a good relationship.

Plan to spend time with your prodigal to reopen the lines of communication. Schedule a special holiday (a skiing or a swimming/boating vacation), doing something together that the child enjoys. Arrangements can be made to have the other children stay with friends, relatives, or a baby-sitter. The goal is to relax the tension between you and the child and to set the stage for a new kind of communication.

A child growing up with siblings sometimes feels like a

wife whose husband practices polygamy. She is one of many wives who never gets the individual attention of her husband. Children crave undivided attention from parents, and a child who is becoming a prodigal is in crucial need of it.

Fred and Marge Sutton found that they both had to miss some days at work, limit their overtime, and make better use of their hours at home in order to reopen communication. Marge also had to stop worrying about whether or not the house was immaculately clean or well-decorated. Parenting may be costly to our personal pleasures and plans; however, we need to be willing to make sacrifices to grow closer to our children.

Tammy Sutton seemed to respond fairly well to this attention; she began talking to her parents and became involved in family projects. Unfortunately, Luke reacted by retreating even further and by voicing complaints about "people poking their noses in my business."

Step Six: Recognize your responsibility to teach your children in the ways of the Lord by listening to, understanding, and commenting on his or her beliefs.

During this first vacation together, plan to listen to your child more than you talk to him or her and ask more questions than you give answers. You want to communicate, "We love you and we accept you. We want to know what you think and who you are." The focus of this vacation is unconditional love, grace, and intimacy.

Parents must not attempt to dictate what the child believes, since this will again halt communication. However, they must feel free to express their viewpoints and the reasons they do not accept the child's position. They must indicate that even if the child believes differently than they do, he or she is loved. If they give their child's viewpoints a respectful and full hearing, the child will probably be willing to listen to them. Intimacy requires that parents understand the child and that the child understands the parents.

During the Suttons' first vacation with Tammy, Fred and Marge found out that their initial hunch was right; her drinking was not an isolated incident. She had gotten drunk at several parties and had been keeping wine in her locker at school for some time. After asking her a lot of questions about her feelings toward them and listening carefully to her answers, the Suttons realized that Tammy had become angry with them several years earlier when they had moved to a new city which was more advantageous for their careers. "You made this move without even thinking about me," Tammy said. "Did it ever occur to you how hard it would be for me to make new friends?"

Fred and Marge Sutton admitted to Tammy that job opportunities had been the major reason for the move. "However, we also thought that more money would allow you kids to go to the college you desire," Fred said.

Both parents apologized for not being more sensitive to Tammy's feelings and told her how sorry they were that she had been hurt.

The time with Luke was not as profitable. Though Luke and his parents enjoyed skiing together, Luke simply would not confide in them. The atmosphere around the home improved some since Luke seemed to appreciate their interest, but neither Fred nor Marge felt that they really knew what Luke was thinking or doing.

These first six steps in developing a biblical parenting strategy involve interaction with your child. The final step in the process is to provide support for you during this difficult time. Although I have listed the steps in numerical order, many of them need to be begun simultaneously.

Step Seven: Seek a source of encouragement and counsel from other Christians who will support your emotional and spiritual needs.

We need to seek the encouragement, counsel, and insight of a pastor or Christian friend who can help us see our situation from a rational and biblical perspective. Sometimes parents set up meetings within their churches, as my pastor friend did when he began "Concerned Parents."

Claudia Arp, the author of *Almost Thirteen*, has organized Mom's Support Groups within churches throughout the country. The appendix to her book gives the specific details of how to begin a Mom's Support Group and suggests activities for the first year's meetings. Paul Lewis, founder of a quarterly newsletter for fathers, *For Dads Only*, used this guide to begin a "Dad's Support Group" in California. Parents could also use these materials to begin a parents' support group.

WHAT DO PARENTS DO IF THE CHILD OPENLY BECOMES A PRODIGAL?

Even if we take these steps to stop our beginning prodigal from becoming destructively rebellious, he or she may not respond to our efforts. Fred and Marge took these constructive steps to head off the prodigal process in their son and daughter. Tammy responded to their efforts, but Luke only drifted farther from them. Eventually he ran away and began living on the streets. Fred and Marge finally learned that he was addicted to drugs.

What should you do if your child becomes openly hostile and engages in illegal activities? The first rule to follow in this situation is again: DON'T PANIC!

As repetitive as that sounds, it is a vital attitude to remember as one deals with prodigal children. Often parents have been trying so hard to change the relationship that they may despair if the situation gets worse rather than better. It's natural to be discouraged and want to give up, but you must not swerve from your covenant strategy.

If you have not been able to get the child in counseling before, try again. However, don't force him or her to participate. In most cases, counseling can only be profitable if the child cooperates. If you have not considered counseling for yourselves before, seek a Christian counselor now so you will be better equipped to handle this difficult relationship.

A prodigal child often attempts to manipulate parents by threatening to drop out of school, by lying, or by using physical force; therefore, parents need to develop good communication between each other so that they can present a united front to their child. Few parents comprehend the potential strain that can be created in their own relationship. They begin to accuse each other for the problems that their child is having. Once the child sees that the parents are divided, he or she will often attempt to exploit this division by playing one parent against the other. Unfortunately marriages are often damaged or destroyed during the prodigal process.

The answer to the question that is the theme of this chapter—Can a prodigal remain at home?—is yes, but only if he or she will begin to respond to the parents' attempts to reach him or her through a biblical parenting strategy. If the prodigal rejects all help and his or her behavior begins to threaten the well-being of the family unit, you will have to consider the temporary separation I suggested earlier in this chapter. In the case of minors this should only be considered if there is a real and significant danger to the emotional, spiritual, or physical health of the siblings or the parents.

What do you do if your child rejects your efforts to reach

him, as Luke did? How do parents respond to a prodigal child's wild living? The next chapter will suggest how a parent can continue to love the prodigal and still reject his wayward actions.

6

How Do I Handle My Prodigal's Wild Living?

September 20, A.D. 30

Dear Diary,

I am becoming increasingly worried about Produs. My good friend Numa was in town yesterday and happened to see Produs in the company of people who are well known as gamblers and prostitutes. While I do not want to make any accusations merely on the basis of association, I do wish I could talk to Produs about his actions. He never confides in me anymore. In fact, I rarely see him. What should I do?

Theo

I first began to counsel Kay Jamison when her husband, Tom, became deeply involved in a non-Christian cult and left the family's church. Tom soon wanted his wife to join his new "church," but Kay resisted. She knew that she would be denying her belief in Christ as God if she joined this group.

Finally, Tom told Kay, "If you loved me, you would join my church. Since you won't I want a divorce."

The Jamison's daughter, Joyce, sided with her mother in the divorce proceedings but Kay was afraid that her daughter felt torn between her mother and father. Her daughter's actions in the next two years confirmed her suspicion.

First, Joyce suddenly decided to leave the dormitory of the Christian college she attended to live in off-campus housing with her roommate. Kay went along with Joyce's decision since Mary, Joyce's roommate, had spent Christmas vacation with the Jamison's during the girls' freshman year.

By the end of her sophomore year, however, Joyce asked to transfer to a state university in the same city as the Christian college.

"All that Christian talk doesn't seem to make a difference in people's lives," she insisted. "I'd rather attend a secular school where people aren't hypocrites."

The fall of her senior year Joyce never called or wrote either Kay or Tom Jamison. Then one evening in November, Joyce called her mother. "It's time you know the truth," she began. "Mary and I are more than just friends. We are lovers." Joyce told her mother that she and Mary were happy together and that she did not intend to stop the relationship. "I hope you understand."

Sometimes a parent's worst fears are realized. Some prodigal children do become involved in every type of vice, heresy, and transgression imaginable, such as:

- alcohol and/or drug addiction
- homosexuality or lesbianism
- promiscuity, extramarital sex
- prostitution

- stealing
- violent crimes, such as murder
- membership in a religious cult
- atheism or agnosticism.

No one can be neutral. Once a person rejects one set of beliefs and values, he or she adopts another philosophy which is reflected by a different lifestyle. Some young people make an intellectual decision to adopt another philosophy or religion, such as the Moonies. Others, like the prodigal son in the story told by Jesus, simply want to be engaged in "wild living." Their rejection of Christian values and beliefs is motivated by nothing more than "the lust of the flesh, the lust of the eyes, and the pride of life" (1 John 2:16), but they are unconsciously adopting a hedonistic philosophy.

A PIG IS A PIG

Unfortunately, even children who engage in the most unorthodox practices may contend that their behavior is not contrary to the Christian faith. For instance, an entire denomination of so-called churches justifies homosexuality and lesbianism. If our children happen to be engaged in this lifestyle, they may join such a church and respond to our pleas for repentance with the rationalization, "Our church says that the Bible never condemns homosexual relations."

Parents need to correct this destructive lie immediately. The Bible does condemn homosexuality and lesbianism. Paul told the Romans that God hates the ungodliness and unrighteousness of men. Then he specifically named these "vile passions": "For even their women exchanged the natural use for what is against nature. Likewise also the men, leaving the natural use of the woman, burned in their lust for one another, men with men committing what is shameful, and receiving in themselves the penalty of their error which was due" (Rom. 1:26-27).

Prodigals who have been raised in Christian homes are particularly prone to try to seek a church that will endorse their activities. They want to "have their cake and eat it, too," as the old saying goes. These prodigals can then be involved in sinful sexual activities and still claim to be "dedicated Christians." Such rationalization keeps them from repentance. They claim to have never left the Christian faith.

Other prodigal children may become involved in a religious cult that uses the name Jesus Christ even though it denies His deity and atonement for our salvation. These prodigals still claim to be Christians; they have just come to a "better understanding of the truth." These children may even try to convert their parents to their newly found faith.

This tendency for children to become associated with cults was widely publicized in the 1970s, and since little is said about it today, some think this is no longer a problem. However, each year millions of Americans, most of whom were raised in mainline Christian denominations, join cults.

Studies done by Dr. Philip G. Zimbardo and Cynthia F. Hartley in the San Francisco Bay area demonstrate some frightening trends. Fifty-four percent of all high school students surveyed in the study had been approached by a member of a cult. And fifty-one percent said they would be willing to go to a cult meeting if invited. Additionally, 3 percent of high school students have been or are currently members of cult groups.[1] Remember that the primary group targeted by cults is not high school students but those in college. Therefore, it is likely that these percentages would be even higher if college students were questioned.

Another study found that 10 percent of all those who attend a meeting of the Unification Church (headed by Sun Yung Moon) stated they wanted to be members. Of these five percent became active members for at least a year, often leaving their education and family to work full time for the organization.[2] Considering that Billy Graham's crusades usually have only 1.5 percent of the audience make a first time profession of faith in Christ, it is clear that the cults are being incredibly effective in their gaining recruits, mainly among the young.[3]

J. Gordon Melton reports that 85 percent of cult members were raised in at least nominally religious homes.[4] Cults seem to have a tendency to attract young people at particular times in their life. College students who are bright and idealistic during times of transition and depression are very vulnerable to becoming members of cults. Those who remain active in a cult six weeks or longer find it difficult to leave the group.[5]

Unfortunately, cult groups are still actively enlisting teenagers and college students while the Christian church is finding it difficult to recruit enough youth pastors to fill the positions that now exist. Dr. Michael D. Longone, Director of the American Family Foundation and cult expert, believes that we might soon be facing an explosion in the growth of cults, as never before seen in this country, because of the Christian church's lack of ministry to young adults.[6]

If Christian parents do not know *why* they believe what they believe, they will be unable to respond to these lies with the truth. Some parents will need to read more about their Christian beliefs and even ask their pastor or minister the questions their children are asking them.

FOUR CRUCIAL ATTITUDES

I suggest four attitudes for parents to adopt as they respond to children who are living as prodigals. This approach will require parents to be patient with their children and to remain committed to them, despite their sins, over a fairly long period of time.

1. Do not focus on the sin, but on the person.

Every unbeliever is engaged in some type of unethical behavior or heretical belief, but when we attempt to reach them, we focus our attention on their salvation through accepting Christ, not on the depravity of their sin. This principle of evangelism does not change when we cross the threshold of our homes. The real focus of our child's problems is the absence of Christ, not his or her sinful deeds, which are only manifestations of that problem.

Joyce Jamison was involved in a lesbian lifestyle, but her real problem was her rejection of Christianity. Her father's actions and the turmoil of the divorce had contributed to this rejection, but she had also had bad dating experiences with "Bible majors" at her school. She had been forced to fight off sexual advances from these "spiritual leaders." Mary, Joyce's roommate and lover, had struggled with many of the same problems of divorce in her family; she, too, had experienced the hypocrisy of "Christian men" who attempted to add her to their list of sexual conquests. These common problems had drawn them close, and then, one day, they crossed the line to become lovers.

Thankfully, Kay Jamison was able to control her emotions the day Joyce told her about their lesbian relationship. "I need to pray about this before I respond to what you are saying," she told her daughter. "I'll talk to you tomorrow." Kay then spent that evening and the next day talking to her pastor, reading portions in the Bible about parenting and fear, and walking in a local park. That evening she called Joyce.

She began their conversation by talking about some of the emotional turmoil she was feeling. Then she said, "Joyce, you know I love you. You also know that the Bible says that lesbianism is a sin. I believe what Paul said in Romans 1. If you don't remember his words, you should read this chapter again. I think you and Mary have made a tragic mistake.

"However, I will try to understand how you feel and why you think this is the right direction for your life. Your choice to become a lesbian does not effect my love for you. In fact, I'd like to have lunch with you next week. It's been so long since we've been together."

Even though Joyce felt a little defensive about Kay's disagreement with her lifestyle, she could hear the love and warmth in her mother's voice. She agreed to meet her mother for lunch the next week.

Kay had accomplished the first step in her parenting strategy: she had not allowed Joyce's declaration to sever the ties between them. She could still communicate God's love to her daughter.

All parents need to strive to maintain a relationship with the child that includes his or her entire life, not just the area of conflict. This area of life will always lead to disagreement and tension. Parents need to keep their concern for their son or daughter foremost in their minds, not their concern about his or her sin. Then they can still communicate unconditional love, which is part of a biblical parenting strategy.

However, as always, this unconditional love does not mean that we will financially support our child's irresponsible behavior. When prodigal children ask parents to pay the bills, the answer should be, "No, I will neither support your new lifestyle nor intervene if you suffer financial difficulties because of your irresponsible actions."

For example, Joyce continued to ask Kay for money for her secular education. Kay had to reply, "Honey, I love you and I always will. You know that I have been willing to help you financially in the past. To show that I still love you, I will send you one more check to help meet your rent.

"After that, you will have to support yourself. You have chosen to abandon your Christian faith and its values. Your lifestyle is in open opposition to all I believe. I cannot support you in good conscience before God."

Kay assured Joyce, "You can always come back home to live as long as Mary does not come with you or visit you." This offer of fellowship promised Joyce that she always had a place of refuge where she could receive help.

2. "Be swift to hear, slow to speak, slow to wrath" (James 1:19).

Jesus warned His disciples that communicating the gospel would not be easy. "Therefore," he advised, "be wise as serpents and harmless as doves" (Matt. 10:16). We must find ways to break down the walls of indifference our prodigal children have built around themselves so we can still have significant and meaningful conversations with them. We need to utilize two principles of good communication:

PREPARE THE STAGE: Choose the right time and place for the conversation.

Kay met her daughter for lunch the next week, then she suggested that they drive to the beach together. Quiet days at the beach and the park had been a part of their relationship since Joyce was a child. Joyce had always loved animals and the out-of-doors. Nothing was more relaxing to both of them than getting away from the city to a natural setting.

OPEN THE DOOR: Make sure you have your child's attention. If not, wait for another opportunity.

Parents must be sure that the prodigal child is really focusing on the conversation. Begin your discussion with a startling statement or a question about one of the child's interests.

I had suggested these principles to Kay during a counseling session, so she had thought about what she might say to Joyce. For a while Kay and Joyce just walked along the beach, stopping every so often to rest and watch the waves lap on the shore. Once, as they were sitting on some rocks overlooking the ocean, Kay asked Joyce, "Are you happy? Really happy, Joyce?"

"Yes," Joyce snapped defensively, "happier than I've ever been!" Realizing the sharp sound of her voice, Joyce paused a moment, then continued in a softer tone. "Don't worry, Mom. I'm fine."

Obviously, Joyce was not going to admit that she sometimes questioned her lifestyle so Kay waited for another opportunity to talk to her. Later, when Kay saw a flock of birds flying overhead, she said, "I have always wondered how birds know when it's time to fly south for the winter. Do you know?"

Since Joyce had enjoyed reading about animals and talking about their habits, she naturally knew the answer to Kay's question. "It's their instinct that drives them south before the cold weather kills them," Joyce responded. Later, when a sea gull and sand crab came over to them, Kay asked Joyce about their habits and how they survived. Over and over again the answer was: "They live by instinctive hungers to go in the direction that helps them survive."

Kay was purposely leading into a spiritual discussion through the side door rather than by a direct assault on Joyce's beliefs. Finally she said, "You know all this talk about instinct reminds me of something I read about human beings this week."

Joyce was naturally curious. "Really, what was it?"

"Well, I was reading a book by St. Augustine, a man who really questioned his religious beliefs. He said he finally realized that there is a hole in every person's soul which can only be satisfied by being filled by God," Kay said. "All this talk about animals' instincts causes me to think that this hole might be the 'God instinct' in man . . . though most of us probably try to satisfy it with other things, I suppose."

The rolling waves, the beauty of the ocean and the shore, all made Joyce more open to talking about the meaning of life. "I wish I could really know God. Not all those theories I learned in school, but really know Him. He seems so far away, so unreal, except in places like this, where He seems so very near."

"I know what you mean," Kay replied. "The power and beauty of the ocean always make me think about the Jesus who had the power to calm the waves of the sea of Galilee and who I believe was the ultimate revelation of God, as you know."

Joyce smiled. "I know, I know. 'The ultimate question of Christ' as we studied in college. Well, Mom, does Jesus love lesbians?"

The question was so direct, Kay was startled. Still she knew that Joyce was using this question to ask many others. Kay took her daughter's hand in hers and responded in a firm voice with the only answer she could. "Yes, He does. He died for them."

The moment was gone as quickly as it came. Joyce did not reply and soon after that she suggested that they had better start to walk back to the car. But Kay hoped that moments such as this would make Joyce begin to re-evaluate her lifestyle.

3. Refuse to argue with your children about their ungodly actions.

A few weeks after their trip to the beach, Joyce called her mother. The beginning of their conversation was casual, yet Joyce's replies were terse. She kept contradicting her mother, no matter what Kay said. Finally, Kay decided to face the tension directly. "I'm sorry you're having a hard day. I pray it gets better."

"I know. I know!" Joyce exploded. "Everything would be okay if I broke up with Mary. God would be happy with me and the world would be magically filled with roses!

"I love Mary," Joyce insisted. "We are happy. Your sexual hangups are just outdated taboos. Mary and I are as normal as everybody else. Only people with small minds—like you—condemn us."

Thankfully, Joyce could not see the tears in Kay's eyes. Instead of trying to justify her position, Kay simply said, "I'm sorry if you think I said something to condemn you. I didn't mean to. I love you and always will.

"Why don't we talk again later. We will only hurt each other if we talk any longer now. I love you, Joyce. Let's talk tomorrow."

Kay hung up the phone before she began to cry. She knew that many things are best left unsaid, especially if their only purpose is to hurt the other person. She had been quick to ask for forgiveness, so their conversation had ended on a positive note. This kept the communication between them open.

4. Be prepared to witness to your children about God's saving grace in Jesus Christ. The real answer to the problem of sin is the gospel.

Parents tend to think that they can evangelize their children with techniques different from those they use to approach other people. For instance, if we were attempting to reach our neighbors with the gospel of Jesus Christ, we would never set the stage by being short-tempered with them or complaining about the condition of their yard. Neither would we try to convince them by lecturing them at great length or by ignoring their questions.

Yet, some of us refuse to discuss any different points of view with our children, and at the same time we demand that they believe exactly what we tell them. Even after our children become adults, we still tend to think that we can dictate what they should believe. Parents need to realize that we cannot send a twenty-one year old to his or her room for doing or saying the wrong thing. We must recognize that adults—or children—will not be badgered into the faith or nagged out of a sinful lifestyle. Many of the ways parents tend to convey values to their children will never produce more than the outward conformity most children adopt. Instead, our children need the same care, concern, and sensitivity as anyone else when we present the gospel. This is especially true of adult prodigals.

As Kay Jamison thought about Joyce in the next days and weeks, she realized that she had never witnessed to her about God's power in her own life. Like many men, her husband Tom had not been much of a Bible student and had never led the family in worship and Bible study. He felt that he was fulfilling the requirements of a Christian parent by taking his daughter to church and living a

114

decent life. Now that her husband had joined a cult and her daughter was involved in a lesbian relationship, Kay realized the importance of Christian teaching and witness.

When they were again having lunch together and reminiscing about Joyce's childhood a few weeks later, Kay felt a little of the old bond between them return. She reached out to take Joyce's hand. In a loving, sincere voice, she softly said, "I'm afraid that I never really told you that my faith is more than just going to church or being good. I feel Christ's presence deep inside me so completely that there can be no doubt that He exists. I know there are good reasons to believe in Jesus and to be committed to Him as my personal Lord and Savior. That's the most important part of my life. Someday I hope you'll be able to see that you need this relationship with Him, too.

"Christ can forgive you and free you from being a lesbian. I love you, Joyce. I want what is best for you."

Parents need to foster a spiritual thirst in their child by demonstrating their own trust in God and the serenity this faith gives them. In the weeks after that luncheon date, Kay continued to talk to Joyce on the phone, meet her for lunch, and even agreed to have dinner with both Joyce and Mary at their apartment one night.

As the three of them were talking after dinner that night, Joyce said to her mom, "You seem to be so adjusted. I don't know how you ever got over the divorce. You really loved Dad, didn't you?"

Kay's eyes filled with tears. "Yes, I loved him, and I guess I always will. But he divorced me when I refused to join his new church.

"I wasn't trying to be stubborn, Joyce, I just couldn't deny that Jesus is God, as they do. It hasn't been easy for me. Yet the Lord has given me a peace and strength I never had before."

Joyce got up from the table and came over to her mother. She put her arms around her and hugged her as they cried together. "I love Daddy, too," she admitted. "I don't know why this ever happened. I need both of you."

"We both need you, too," Kay answered. "You don't need to choose between us, just because we are divorced. I don't mind if you spend time with your dad."

Shortly after that evening Joyce came home for a weekend. As Kay and Joyce were looking through the family album together that Saturday night, Joyce began to cry. "I do feel guilty about my relationship with Mary," she admitted. "Oh, Mom, I know I've sinned. What am I going to do?"

Joyce knew the answer to her own question. Certainly she'd studied salvation in her courses at the Christian college. Still she needed someone else to walk through the steps of forgiveness with her.

"You know that we all sin, Joyce," Kay began. "Not one of us is good enough to live with God, so Christ died for our sins. You have to confess to Him and ask His forgiveness."

Kay and Joyce bowed their heads and together they prayed for the Lord to forgive Joyce. Kay hugged her daughter at the end of this prayer and for a long while they sat there together.

"When your dad told me that I had to leave my faith in Jesus or be faced with a divorce, I realized that I had to make a clear decision. Did I love Christ more than I loved your dad? Would I depend on my husband to provide for me or Christ? It was then that I recognized that I could not live for other people or depend on them to make me happy, since they are sinners just as I am.

"At that point I gave my life to Someone I can count on, to Someone who deserves my trust since He's perfect. I told the Lord, 'Whatever you want for me is what I want.'

Now I'm truly in His hands. I knew that if I said I believed in Him, I had to give Him my total loyalty.

"That's what I think you need to do. You need to understand that the question before you is 'Who do I love more, Jesus or Mary?' That's a part of salvation that many of us forget. We accept Christ as Savior but we forget that we must also make Him Lord of our lives if we are to truly enjoy His forgiveness and salvation. Here, let me show you this passage in the Bible that helped me as I struggled with what I would say to your father when he told me to join the cult or lose him." Kay turned to Matthew 10:37–39.

> He who loves father or mother more than Me is not worthy of Me. And he who loves son or daughter more than Me is not worthy of Me. And he who does not take his cross and follow after Me is not worthy of Me. He who finds his life will lose it, and he who loses his life for My sake will find it.

As Kay and Joyce read this passage together they both cried. What Kay said truly made sense to Joyce. She had watched her mother in the last few years and had seen the difference in her life. Joyce knew that the only way she could change her lifestyle was to make the same commitment. That night she did so. The next day she went back to her apartment to pack her clothes and say goodbye to Mary.

Many parents have never learned to share the gospel with others. I always suggest the steps that we use in Evangelism Explosion, which are in the appendix on page 00. Here you will find our outline for presenting the message of salvation and an example of how I use this outline in my conversation with another person.

In evangelizing their children, most parents will want

to set forth the Christian position, urge their children to repent, and point to Christ as the answer, as Kay did. The issue of sin should be discussed within the framework of God's love, Christ's death and resurrection, repentance, faith, lordship, and forgiveness. This approach is biblical since it is patterned after God's relationship to those who are involved in a sinful lifestyle. On the one hand God stands firm in demanding holiness, while on the other He reaches out to the sinner with love and grace.

Kay's patient response to Joyce's prodigal behavior was used by God as a channel of His grace to deliver her daughter from a wayward lifestyle. God can use you in the same way if you prepare yourself to share the gospel and pray to be used by the Holy Spirit in a sensitive manner to touch your child's heart for God.

7

What Do I Do If My Prodigal Runs Away?

Dear Dad:

This note is to tell you that I am leaving once and for all. I couldn't tell you in person because I knew that you would try to stand in my way. Farm life is not for me, and you just don't seem to understand or care about how I feel, only about your stupid farm. I'm sure Judd will always be with you, so I doubt if you will miss me much.

Goodbye,
Produs

Chad and Terri Tremain had tried to be good parents to their daughter Beth, yet they knew she was troubled. She had attended Christian school for three years, yet now she fought with them constantly about returning to public school. Sometimes she would skip school altogether to emphasize how unhappy she was. "I'm tired of all that religion," she would yell when her parents confronted her. "We're not allowed to have any fun there."

But the real reason was never mentioned. Beth was dating a boy from the local public high school. Chad and Terri knew Beth wanted to be near him at school as well as after school. This was the exact opposite of what they wanted. Beth's boyfriend never went to church, and he consistently denounced her Christian beliefs. He even made cynical remarks about the existence of God to Beth's parents.

Beth began spending greater and greater amounts of time alone in her room, listening to her stereo. Sometimes Chad and Terri would not see her until they went to her room at ten o'clock to tell her to turn off the stereo and get ready for bed. Though they missed talking to her, this uneasy truce seemed to be better than the constant fighting. Maybe she will outgrow this stage, they reasoned.

None of these problems prepared the Tremains for the morning Terri went to Beth's room to awaken her for school and found her bed empty. Beth had run away from home.

Millions of parents face the crisis of their teenager running away from home to either live on the street or with "friends." Studies of students of different high schools show that an estimated 10 to 17 percent of all teenagers in the United States have run away from home. Since the current adolescent population is approximately twenty million, somewhere between two and four million teenagers have, at one time or another, been runaways.[1]

In addition to these teenage runaways, many adult children who have reached the legal age of eighteen escape from their families. Sometimes this break is dramatic, full of angry accusations, slammed doors, and squealing tires. Other times the rejection is masked by the normal process of growing up. Some young people who get married right out of high school are not only motivated by love for their fiance, but are consciously or unconsciously attempting to escape from the influence and lifestyle of their parents. Other young people choose to go to a college in a state as far away from home as possible. Since it is normal for children to move away from home and establish their own lives after high school, this physical move is not recognized by the parents as a symbol of parent/child conflict. After six months or so, however, the parents realize that their children have not only moved out of the house, but out of the family's lifestyle and faith.

SOME HAVE REASON TO RUN

I must honestly say that at times the child's action is justified. Some parents have created environments that are oppressive and even abusive. One study estimated that nearly 40 percent of all teenage runaways say they were subjected to either sexual, physical, or verbal abuse at home. Other teenagers were neglected, simply not given the essential physical needs. Still others could not cope with the problems and emotional turmoil created by an alcoholic parent or parents. As we saw in chapter 4, the Scriptures warn parents not to raise their children in a way that will arouse their anger, but in a godly manner. Obviously some parents in Bible times did not raise their children according to God's laws.

The institution of the family is under a particularly heavy attack from the many people who promote immoral or amoral conduct in our society, and the principles of good parenting are practiced by all too few. Children often equate the parents' tangled life with their profession of Christian faith. "If that's what Christianity is all about" they think, "I don't want any part of it." They reject Christian teachings and values based on the lives of parents who never demonstrated their beliefs consistently.

What if you are one of those parents? Then you need to repent of your inconsistent lifestyle and your sins. Admit your mistakes to your children, and ask them not to reject Christianity because of your poor example.

OTHERS HAVE NO REASON

There is another side to this coin, however. Some experts estimate that perhaps 60 percent of teenage runaways were not abused physically, sexually, or verbally by their parents. This figure probably also holds true for the adult runaways, too.[3]

Many runaways come from homes where parents have been doing a reasonably good job of raising the children, attempting to demonstrate love and striving to provide for their physical, emotional, and spiritual needs. Phyllis and David York and Ted Wachteel, who founded TOUGH-LOVE, a group to help parents deal with prodigal children, feel strongly that parents need to realize that some prodigals run just to party:

> There are other kids out there, not running away from something, but running to something. Something they call partying. They come from families that care about them, from loving homes: wealthy, middle-class, and poor of every race. Like a cab driver in Mississippi who told us, "I jus' don' know. My daughter says she don' believe in Jesus no more and she's jus' runnin' wild. The wife and I are near goin' crazy." And the film executive in California: "I'm desperate. My kid comes and goes. We've gone the route: psychiatrist, counselors, special schools. Nothing seems to help. His friends all look like bums and he fits in with them like a glove. We're scared to death of how he'll end up." Families who fear the dangers of their kids' choices, while their kids see only the excitement and fun. Kids who are busy partying, doing dope, skipping school, shoplifting, hitchhiking, screwing around, and making believe they are adults.[4]

The parents of these children find it hard to understand why their children have rejected their Christian values and abandoned their parents. They are filled with self-doubt, confusion, guilt, anger, and hurt.

How can parents deal with these emotions? Is there any effective way to keep these feelings from driving the parents into depression and despair?

I always go back to that same key principle: DO NOT PANIC!

Unfortunately we often project the "worst case scenario" onto the imaginary screen of the future and accept this scenario as a foregone conclusion. We instantly think that our children will be killed or raped, become prostitutes or drug addicts, when they may actually be hiding at a friend's house, having sneaked through a window that was left ajar.

Once panic sets in, we are often so upset we do not consider our options. We either do not want to hear about any possible solutions since we feel the situation is hopeless or we take desperate risks to relieve the pressure, regardless of how great the odds are against these actions ever succeeding.

Chad and Terri Tremain reacted the first way. They told me they were sure Beth would die from an overdose of drugs or be forced into prostitution because she had left home with only the seventy dollars from her savings account and had no way to earn a living.

"She's so angry with us," Terri said, "that we will never hear from her again."

For the first few days after Beth left, the Tremains would not listen to any biblical counsel. They shot down every possible solution I suggested which would have benefited both themselves and their child. They told me, "We've already tried that and it didn't work." They made it very clear that they were too emotionally upset to explore any rational solutions to their problem.

Another couple I counseled, Bob and Jean Woodward,

took the second approach. They had lost complete control of their son, Tony, who came and went as he pleased. Although they cared for their son in every way possible, he continually accused them of not loving him. Then one Saturday afternoon they returned home early from shopping and discovered Tony in bed with a girl who was living on the street. She was the first of a parade of girls over several months. When Bob Woodward finally confronted Tony about his sexual encounters, Tony threatened to leave home and head for California. Then he actually began packing his bags.

Bob and Jean panicked. They pleaded with him to stay and apologized for being too hard on him. Tony said he needed "space" and that he just could not handle the hassles of living at home under his parents' thumbs. So to keep him close and off the streets, and to show their love, Bob and Jean offered to buy him a condominium, a BMW, and arranged to give him a healthy monthly allowance. It doesn't take a psychologist to figure out how Tony responded. He took the condo, BMW, and money. His lifestyle, though, became even more rebellious and sinful. After all, how would you respond if your parents rewarded you for rejecting their authority?

Parents must remember that when they panic they react much like investors who become hysterical when their stocks fail. Some despair, go into depression, and do nothing at all to recoup their loss. Others suddenly become like gamblers who have been on a losing streak—they put "everything on the line" in a frantic hope of winning their losses back. Neither reaction is a rational response, yet all too many times highly educated, intelligent, and mature businessmen do just that. The reason is *panic*. As parents, we are prone to the same pressures when we fear losing the most precious treasure of our lives: our children.

Faith, rather than panic, is the proper response. King Solomon, one of the wisest men who ever lived, once said that wisdom is found by being cautious and by correctly understanding all the facts. When we make decisions in a calm, prudent, and biblical manner, we know we are acting wisely.

When I tell people this, they respond, "It's easy enough to say we shouldn't panic, but I can't help panicking in these circumstances."

I know exactly how they feel. We all face events and decisions that tempt us to panic. Yet the Bible teaches us that we *can* maintain a positive, prudent attitude in the midst of crisis.

THREE KEY PRINCIPLES

I always suggest three key principles to help parents deal with the natural panic they feel:

1. Every circumstance of life is ultimately used by God for our good, to instill Christlike attitudes in us.

I often quote Romans 8:28 to people who doubt this first principle, like Chad Tremain: "We know that all things work together for good to those who love God, to those who are the called according to His purpose."

Naturally, Chad had difficulty understanding how any good could come from his daughter's running away. I told him some of the ideas I will share with you in Chapter 8, "What Do I Do When My Prodigal 'Bottoms Out?' " Then I said, "Any time we doubt that God wants the best for us, we need to look at Jesus' death on the cross. God bankrupted heaven by giving His only Son to suffer for our sins, once and for all.

"Surely if God were to refrain from doing something good for us, it would have been sacrificing His Son, Jesus

Christ. Yet God did not hold back this gift of infinite worth. Therefore, we can be assured that He will not hold back *anything* that is good for us."

Chad had never thought of the cross in this way, and the reality of God's great sacrifice helped him to see that he could trust God to be in control, despite the seeming hopelessness of their situation.

2. Rejection by family members may be part of the life of faith.

Part of Chad and Terri's problem was that their daughter had decided to reject the gospel and wanted to follow another way of life. Jesus predicted this rejection. In fact, He Himself was rejected and misunderstood by His earthly family until after His resurrection.

One time His mother, brothers, and sisters came to rescue Him from the crowds, thinking He had gone mad from trying to help so many people. Jesus made it clear to them that His loyalty to God's kingdom came before His loyalty to His family. When one of the disciples told Him that His mother and brothers were waiting to see Him, He pointed to His disciples and said, "Here are my mother and my brothers! For whoever does the will of My Father in heaven is my brother and sister and mother." (See Matt. 12:46–50; John 7:1–5.)

3. We cannot predict the future based on the present.

Fear turns into panic because we assume that today's bad circumstances will continue and/or intensify in the future. Jesus warned us about worrying about tomorrow. He said, "Therefore do not worry about tomorrow, for tomorrow will worry about its own things. Sufficient for the day is its own trouble" (Matt. 6:34).

When I mentioned this verse to Chad, he seemed relieved. He soon memorized the passage word for word, the first time he had ever memorized Scripture.

God's Word does not allow us the luxury of sinful depression based on vain, pessimistic speculations about the future. Instead the Scriptures call us to react with hope, placing our faith and trust in the love of God and His plan for our child's life.

Parents must remind themselves that only God knows the future—and He does not reveal it to us. Often our worries never come true, as in the Tremain's case. Two weeks after Beth left, they received a call from her. She had finally gone to her aunt's house a few hundred miles away, and her aunt refused to let her stay unless she called home. God was indeed working for good through this situation, because Beth's aunt was able to convince her to return home. She was also able to witness to Beth about the Christian faith.

These three dynamic and living principles of Scripture will help anyone who faces a crisis to bring his or her feelings of panic under control.

Parents can also be held captive by one of two other emotions at this time, which must be dealt with: either false guilt or self-righteous rationalization. Neither of these responses is constructive.

FALSE GUILT OR SELF-RIGHTEOUSNESS

False guilt, the response parents often have when they first realize their child is a prodigal, will often occur again when a child leaves home. Parents will be prone to relive their entire relationship with their children in their minds, jumping on any number of innocent episodes and dialogues as the reason for their child's desperate action. Many parents try to be "Monday morning quarterbacks"; they blame themselves for not being able to see the negative influences of their every action. Reliving past events only tortures their minds and souls with a tremendous amount of psychologically induced guilt.

On the other hand, some parents respond to the prodigal's leaving home with the opposite reaction of justifying themselves. Again they review the past, but with the purpose of commending themselves and condemning their children.As we all know, in most cases there is some responsibility for a situation on both sides. Usually, no one is totally wrong, and no one entirely right—so this approach is absolutely wrong.

It is extremely inconsistent for parents who claim to be Christians to take a self-righteous and condemning attitude toward their children. In a spiritual sense we have *all* been "prodigal children" who have strayed from our heavenly Father. Only because of God's love and patience with *His* prodigal children is it possible for us to be forgiven and restored to God's family through faith in Jesus Christ. Since God has had such patience, love, mercy, and compassion on us, we also need to demonstrate these qualities.

God's heart was broken when mankind chose sin and rebellion over His love and care. Every caring parent of a prodigal knows to some extent how He feels. Yet, even in the midst of this heartbreak and sorrow, we must not give up believing in God, loving our offspring, and trusting that, by God's grace, they will return to Him.

Once we have controlled our panic and avoided the dangers of self-guilt and justification, we should respond as the father in Jesus' story did when his son ran away. He calmly and patiently waited for the child to return!

This father felt the same emotions you feel. He was grieved that his son despised him so much that he had to run away from home, but he knew that a prodigal cannot be coerced. The son or daughter must make his or her own decision to return home physically and spiritually.

A difficult wait, but one which is always worthwhile! Every morning and every evening after the son left, this father probably walked to a high place and looked out over the countryside to see if his son might be coming home. He had faith, love, and hope.

We must do what we can to find our children, but we must also realize, as this father did, that we cannot force them to be part of our family. We can continue to love them, pray for them, and be concerned for their well-being, but we must wait patiently for them. God is calling us to replace the images of doom in our minds with the vision of our children back home again.

8

What Do I Do When My Prodigal "Bottoms Out"?

Dear Diary:

I must admit things have not gone exactly as I planned. I figured that I had enough money to last a lifetime, but it was all gone before I knew it. Then the depression came. All those "party friends" of mine couldn't spare me a dime to get something to eat.

At times I think about my father: his way of life, and the warnings he gave me about what would happen if I acted irresponsibly. Boy! He sure called this one.

If I had any sense I would quit this lousy pig job and go home. It's hard to admit, but I was wrong.

Produs

After Joe Evans entered his freshman year in high school, he seemed to withdraw from his parents. Lucille and Ed Evans suspected that he was struggling with the normal high school problems: fitting in with a group, finding a girl friend, and adjusting to the more difficult subjects and more intensive home work.

Time and again Lucille and Ed separately asked him,

"How are things going, son? Can we do something to help you?"

Instead of talking with his parents after dinner, as he always had, Joe spent most of his time in his room, listening to music through his stereo headset.

The Evanses noticed that Joe's buddies from church—Eric and Jim—never came over to the house anymore. Neither did anyone else. It was almost as if Joe didn't want his parents to know his new friends. When Ed Evans asked his son about Eric and Jim, Joe nonchalantly replied, "I don't see them much anymore." Then he added, as if anticipating his dad's next question, "We're in different classes. It's a big school, you know."

Late one afternoon, Joe came home from school drunk. His dad confronted him, but Joe just mumbled, "Some guys had beer outside school. They asked me to try some. No big deal, Dad."

Ed Evans tried to get his son to tell him who had the beer, but Joe would not reply. The conversation ended with Ed grounding Joe for two weeks.

The next morning, Ed called the principal, but he knew nothing about the incident. Then Ed contacted me to see if I could help. I suggested that Norm Wise, one of the young counselors on my staff, take Joe out for pizza. "Maybe Joe will talk to Norm."

Norm and Joe went out for pizza the next week and met a couple of other times in the next few months. Norm told me that Joe would tell him very little, since he resented his family calling in a counselor. "Still I sense that Joe has some real problems," Norm said.

In the next months the tension increased. Joe argued constantly with his parents, came home later and later at night, and showed no real sign of remorse when he was punished for staying out beyond his curfew. He was so sullen and withdrawn and looked so hung over all the time that his parents suspected drugs. "No way," Joe replied when they confronted him with their suspicion.

Then one afternoon in the spring of Joe's freshman year, I received an urgent call from Ed. "Joe overdosed on drugs at school. Lucille and I are in the emergency room. Could you meet us here?" Ed asked. "The doctor said Joe might not make it."

By the time I got to the hospital the police were talking to the Evanses. "We were making a routine drug check of school lockers," the lieutenant told Ed and Lucille. "We think your son saw us, and took all the pills in a bottle he had in his locker so we wouldn't find them.

"Within minutes Joe was climbing the walls from the effects of God-only-knows what mixture of drugs. He had to be subdued so we could get him to the hospital," the lieutenant explained.

By God's grace, Joe did not die that day.

When Norm Wise and I visited him the next day, Joe gave a sheepish smile and admitted, "I guess I blew it!"

"Yeah, almost for eternity," Norm replied. He stayed with Joe most of that afternoon and they had their first heart-to-heart talk.

Over the next two weeks, as Joe recovered in the hospital, Norm and I were his only visitors besides his parents. His drug buddies had not even phoned, and when he called them, they hung up. They wanted nothing to do with him now that the police knew he was involved with drugs. Norm and Joe talked about how fragile such friendships are, and together they discussed the story of the prodigal son whose friends also deserted him.

Joe's story is all too typical. Many children who reject their parents' Christian values soon learn that a life dedicated to the wrong principles has a heavy price tag.

THE PIGPEN: THEN AND NOW

The prodigal son's experience in the pigpen is one of the most forceful images in all literature. I talked a little about this pigpen in the second chapter of this book. Let's look at the prodigal son's situation a little more closely now.

When Moses established the laws governing the Jewish people, he declared that touching a pig, or slaughtering a pig, was a transgression of God's law, which made a person ceremonially unclean (see Deut. 14:8; Lev. 11:7).

The prophet Isaiah called Israel to account for eating the flesh of pigs (see Isa. 65:4) and committing other sins, worshipping idols and evil spirits. Isaiah said that anyone who sacrificed pigs in worship was committing an abomination (see Isa. 66:3, 17). Pigs were sacrificed in some pagan ceremonies, but this practice was blasphemy for Jews.

Antiochus Ephiphanes, king of Syria, the continual enemy of Israel, openly defied and ridiculed the Israelites after he conquered Jerusalem by erecting a new altar to the pagan god Jupiter Olympius on top of the sacred altar. Then he sacrificed pigs on his pagan altar, an act that was just a part of his massive persecution of the Jews at this time. He hung Jewish mothers who circumcised their male children in obedience to God's command on crosses to die, with their children chained around their necks.[1]

Antiochus killed anyone who dared to have a copy of the Torah and destroyed every copy of God's Word that he could find. The symbol of this monstrous persecution was the sacrifice of pigs. Swine became as repulsive to the Jews as the Nazi swastika would later become. For these reasons the Jewish teacher of the law declared, "Cursed is the man who tends swine."

Obviously the young man in Jesus' story had reached the lowest straits of society when he accepted a job tending pigs. He had truly "bottomed out."

The conditions of modern pigpens differ, but they are just as degrading. Each year the counseling staff of our radio and television ministries, Coral Ridge Ministries, receives thousands of letters, filled with cries of help from prodigals who have "bottomed out" when they:

- Are abused by some "lover" who uses them as a punching bag.
- Are so addicted to drugs that they are unable to function normally.
- Are fired from their jobs because their wild living has made them unproductive and irresponsible.
- Are diagnosed as having AIDS, which has been contracted because of promiscuity or drug abuse.
- Are plagued by suicidal thoughts because nothing gives them the "high" they were looking for when they first began their ungodly lifestyles.

As we respond to the letters from these prodigals and pray for their needs, I always remember that their suffering is not without purpose, but may be a part of God's working in their lives.

Why the Pigpen?

As parents, we sometimes have a hard time understanding why our children have to suffer as they do. We become fearful of their health and even their lives, yet we must commit our children to God in the knowledge that He is able to use these bad factors to bring them to a true faith. As C. S. Lewis, a great scholar and man acquainted with grief, once said: "God whispers to us in our pleasures, speaks in our conscience, but shouts in our pains: it is his megaphone to rouse a deaf world."[2]

Even as we weep for our children when they find themselves at the "end of their ropes," we must never allow ourselves to despair, for we know that God is at work in their lives. Often the prodigal will repent, just as the prodigal son in Jesus' story did.

The prodigal son's downfall began with an event that was entirely outside the range of human control, a famine in the land. This occurence is an act of nature, under God's control, and men historically see it as a physical reminder that God is angry with their transgressions and will judge them unless they repent. If the famine had not occurred at the same time that the prodigal son ran out of money, he might not have been forced to accept a job as lowly as tending pigs. The natural disaster contributed to the son's eventual repentance.

The same may be true of the "famines" our children face. While providence may sometimes seem to be working against the prodigal, God can turn the problem into potential. Parents need to maintain this positive perspective of the "bottoming-out" process so they can effectively minister to their children.

Prodigals can sometimes be the victims of other people's sins (as in instances of rape or theft), but most times their woes are self-inflicted. If the prodigal son had gone to the city, used part of his inheritance to start a good business, and saved a part, the famine would not have been such a life-shattering experience. Ultimately, the prodigal was tending pigs because of his own sinful acts and he realized this. When anyone devotes his life to fulfilling his uncontrolled desires and lusts, the result will always involve psychological, physical, and spiritual problems. Prodigals simply "reap what they sow," as Proverb 22:8 and Galatians 6:7–8 predict.

The Goal of Suffering in the Pigpen

How should parents pray for their children once they begin to reap what they have sown? I suggest that we ask God to use his megaphone to reach their hearts so they begin to reconsider their lives. Jesus described this process as "coming to himself."

Dr. Archibald Thomas Robertson points out that some scholars believe that Plato, the great Greek philosopher, used this phrase "to come to oneself" for the moment a person became "redeemed." Jesus speaks of the prodigal as though he has been out of his head and now has come to see reality.

Suddenly the prodigal son knew he had been asleep—the life he thought was real (sex and drunkenness) was not real. No real joy, no real friends, no real inner peace. Nothing. If he continued to follow this lifestyle, death from starvation was certain.

Every person comes to himself when he says, "What a fool I've been." This is what happened to Joe. He told Norm Wise, "You know, I've been thinking. I was a fool to get involved with drugs, but I really believed it was the only way I could get friends. Then, after I was hooked, I thought it was the only way to be happy.

"I thought I had everything and life was great. Then, when I nearly . . . ," Joe's voice choked up as he thought about his experience, "died, and all my friends deserted me, I realized that if I kept living that way I was on a quick road to hell. I really messed up, but I'm sorry, and I want God and my parents to forgive me. I don't care what I have to do, I want to straighten out."

Humility is another element in "coming to one's self," as Joe's statement shows. Every prodigal who has experienced a change of heart is ready to do whatever is necessary to straighten out his life, just as the prodigal son was ready to be a servant in his own father's house.

This change of attitude is crucial. People make outward changes for a variety of reasons, but a lasting change only occurs when there has been a radical change of heart. The Bible calls this repentance. The prodigal son experienced a deep realization of the nature of sin: "I have sinned against heaven and you," he admitted. John Calvin, the great Protestant reformer, in commenting on this passage, said, "all the miseries which we endure are a profitable invitation to repentance."

Unfortunately, today many prodigals (like Lisa Hoover, a teenager I counseled) feel they are already "saved" and have no need to "come to themselves," even though they are involved in the most ungodly lifestyles. They claim Jesus as their Savior (saving them from their sins by dying on the cross) but they have never accepted Him as Lord of their lives, which commits them to a life of discipleship.

Lisa Hoover had "accepted Christ as Savior" when she attended a youth retreat in her junior year of high school. Her church took the position that a person first accepts Jesus as Savior, then, as a person grows in faith, he or she later accepts Him as Lord. The church even maintained that "churches who teach that a person has to accept Christ as Lord as well as Savior before he or she can be saved are adding works to salvation."

This doctrine keeps a lot of prodigals from facing their behavior and repenting of it. Since Lisa never accepted Christ as Lord of her life, she never rejected her ungodly behavior. She occasionally got drunk, as she always had, at the same time that she actively attended church and studied the Bible.

Once Lisa went to college, she stopped attending church and studying the Bible. She started smoking marijuana, got drunk nearly once a month, and went to bed with a few of her boyfriends. Still Lisa thought she was saved.

One day an old friend from her church youth group convinced Lisa to go to a Bible study. The text for that evening was Galatians 6:7–8: "Do not be deceived, God is not mocked; for whatever a man sows, that he will also reap. For he who sows to his flesh will of the flesh reap corruption, but he who sows to the Spirit will of the Spirit reap everlasting life."

During his message the minister proclaimed, "Clearly the apostle Paul said, 'If you live a life of wild living as the prodigal, and never repent, then do not be misled, you will go to hell. But if you turn from your sins, call out to Christ for forgiveness as the Holy Spirit is convicting you to do, and begin to live for Jesus, you will have everlasting life."

Lisa felt uncomfortable. She recognized that she had been planning to live for herself and then depend on Jesus as her "fire insurance" for eternity. Now, it seemed that this plan would not work.

"If I am continually choosing to sin and have never accepted Jesus as Lord, then I am not really saved," Lisa realized. She spoke with the minister for hours after the Bible study and finally made the decision to submit to Christ as the Lord of her life.

True conversion means turning away from living for sin and turning to Jesus to live for Him. The Holy Spirit must touch our hearts, force us to face ourselves honestly in our sin, and then create in us the desire to make a change. Lisa is now the mother of two small children and a godly, dedicated disciple. For her, it was vital to understand that she could not use Jesus as "fire insurance." She realized that to have salvation she must not only fully trust in Jesus as Savior, but she must also want to follow Him as Lord. This revelation changed her life.

Lisa Hoover is just one of millions of prodigals who think that a person doesn't need to change an attitude toward sin to be saved. Yet true biblical faith is not merely an acceptance of Jesus as some type of eternal life insurance, but as our prophet, priest, and king:

- as our Prophet: the God incarnate who came to teach the truth about God and life (submission of our minds)
- as our Priest: the Savior who paid for our sins and gave us eternal life (submission of our trust)
- as our King: the absolute ruler of our lives (submission of our wills).

A true saving faith always includes an about face, a turning away from sin and a turning toward God and His revelation in Jesus Christ. Parents must share the truth of Scripture, which Paul summarized in Galatians 5:19–21, with their children:

Now the works of the flesh are evident, which are: adultery, fornication, uncleanness, licentiousness, idolatry, sorcery, hatred, contentions, jealousies, outbursts of wrath, selfish ambitions, dissensions, heresies, envy, murders, drunkenness, revelries, and the like; of which I tell you beforehand, just as I also told you in time past, that those who practice such things will not inherit the kingdom of God.

This passage makes it clear that those who continue in a disobedient lifestyle of sin and still claim Christ as Savior are living in a "fool's paradise." True faith always accepts Jesus as *both* Lord and Savior. It cannot be otherwise.

Parents must be careful as they talk to their children about this passage of Scripture. We do not want our children to feel as if we are condemning them (and, in fact, we have no right to make the final judgment about anyone's salvation). We must share this Scripture with them in an attitude of love and legitimate concern. We must tell them, "We do not know what you believe in your heart, but your actions are those that stem from unbelief not faith. Examine your heart honestly before God and ask yourself if Christ is truly in your life. We do not want you to have a false confidence in your salvation and then find yourself sorry for eternity." (See 2 Cor. 13:5).

We must also be careful not to confuse our children's struggle with one particular sin as a sign that they lack all faith. The Timmons, parents I once counseled, were able to avoid this error. Their teenage daughter Carolyn was active in her young people's group, yet she began to have a drinking problem. She confessed her drunkenness to her parents and the church but continued to struggle with her problem. She hated her sin, but at times, she allowed it to control her.

The Timmons did not question the sincerity of Carolyn's faith since the rest of her life was consistent with her Christian beliefs. They decided to make an agreement with Carolyn: "If you drink too much, you are to call us so we can drive you home." The Timmons were able to protect their daughter from one of the worst consequences of her actions—accidental death from drunken driving—as she struggled to overcome her addiction. After receiving Christian counseling, Carolyn gained greater self-control. She has stayed sober for several years now.

If your child has a desire to grow in faith, demonstrates repentance about a number of issues, and continues to go to church, but he or she is still occasionally trapped by a gross sin (such as drugs or sex), you need to recognize that he or she is going through the normal battle with sin that is common to all Christians. In such cases you need to encourage and help your child as he or she battles with moral weakness. At times you need to encourage the child to seek counseling. As long as the child continues to fight the sin and demonstrates true sorrow for transgressions, there is no reason for you, or your child, to doubt the sincerity and reality of his or her faith.

BUT MY CHILD'S AT THE TOP, NOT THE BOTTOM!

Some children do not bottom out as Joe did. Instead they seem to prosper because they exercise some restraint and use common sense by not mixing their behavior with their working environment. Indeed, if a prodigal is an achiever who has a very materialistic outlook, he or she may do quite well financially. "I've never been happier," they may tell their Christian parents, using their secular success as proof of the validity of their moral choices.

The writer of Psalm 73 tried to understand how people who have chosen to reject God can seem to be materially successful and happy. He said:

When I thought how to understand this,
It was too painful for me—until I went into the sanctuary of God;
Then I understood their end.
Surely You set them in slippery places;
You cast them down to destruction.
Oh, how they are brought to desolation, as in a moment!
They are utterly consumed with terrors!
As a dream when one awakes,
So Lord when You awake,
You shall despise their image.

Psalm 73:16–20

Though a man may prosper every day of his life, he must face the judgment of God at his death. Suffering in this life is not the greatest difficulty a person can face; suffering for all eternity is true hopelessness.

141

Sometimes a prodigal may be brought to repentance through the outpouring of God's blessings. That is the way it was in my life. I was successful in business, had a good income, and was fairly content with life. Yet, this goodness caused me to seek God.

I knew life was good, but I also realized life was too short. *Surely,* I thought, *there must be a way to remain happy beyond this life.*

Sometimes I would stand on a bridge over the Hillsborough River. As I saw the water flowing underneath, I thought, *That water has been here since long before I was born. And it's going to be here long after I die. Surely, I am greater than a body of water. There must be something more!*

Thoughts like this led me to investigate God's promise of eternal life. The Scripture talks about this process in Romans 2:4: "Don't you realize how patient he is being with you? Or don't you care? Can't you see that he has been waiting all this time without punishing you, to give you time to turn from your sin? His kindness is meant to lead you to repentance" (TLB).

God can use either adversity or prosperity to influence a prodigal's heart. As parents we must pray that our prodigal children will "come to themselves" and experience true, bibilical repentance. Our part in this is to pray earnestly, and when our prodigal hits bottom, be ready to clearly present the true gospel of Christ. We do have hope. God is able to clear our child's thinking, change his or her heart, and turn the prodigal back toward home.

9

What Do I Do When My Prodigal Returns Home?

Dear Produs,

I am glad that in your last letter you were beginning to see some of the mistakes you had made. I rejoice at how God is working in your life, even though I am sorry that you have had to suffer through such hard circumstances.

Remember, my son, I love you. Whenever you feel like returning home, you are welcome. Write again soon.

Love,
Dad

Parents like Ralph and Helen Harrison, who struggle with their prodigal child's behavior over many years, often become desperate. The Harrisons, whose daughter, Linda, had become hopelesly hooked on drugs, counseled with me every other month when Linda was away from home. When she returned, they began frequent counseling. The last two times she'd been home she had argued incessantly with her parents and each time had returned to a life of sexual promiscuity, drunkenness, and drug abuse.

One day in 1986 they came to see me. Helen cried as she

told me about Linda's recent arrest for drug abuse, which, as always, had made Linda decide to come home to dry out. "Dr. Kennedy," Helen said, "I just don't think I can take much more. Every time she comes home I hope she will straighten out. Then she begins to take drugs again—and she leaves."

"What can we do?" Ralph asked. "Do we have to take her back? We're stuck on an emotional roller coaster. When is enough, enough?"

Many parents find themselves in the similar, strange position, wanting their prodigal to return but not knowing how to handle the situation. Every parent of a prodigal faces extremely hard, emotional decisions when the prodigal returns to the family circle. Parents must prepare themselves for this day before it ever occurs.

HOW TO PREPARE FOR THE PRODIGAL CHILD'S RETURN

As the years drag on, parents can be overwhelmed with personal pain, which develops into anger and resentment. These attitudes can be brought on by what Professor Joseph Procaccini of Loyola College in Baltimore calls parent burnout. Parents who erroneously accept the blame for their children's failing and isolate themselves from the love and support of other members of their family, experience this "burnout."[1] Parents must prepare for the prodigal's return by trying to avoid parent burnout and by learning to trust their child, though not blindly.

Avoid Parent Burnout

Ralph Harrison's question, "When is enough, enough?" indicated a severe case of parent burnout. As he looked at the toll Linda's behavior had taken on him and his wife over a period of eight years, he knew he would have trouble controlling his resentment when Linda came home.

In counseling I helped Ralph to take three important steps to learn to resolve his anger and use his emotions constructively. First, Ralph had to accept the responsibility for these emotions. Linda had not forced him to become angry. He had chosen to react in anger rather than learn to control his anger. He had to realize that the "anger of man" does not work the righteousness of God. As Linda began to be more combative during her third stay at home, Ralph had to leave the room in the middle of an argument to keep from saying or doing anything he would regret later.

Secondly, Ralph needed to realize that the Holy Spirit motivates a different kind of anger (a "righteous anger") and can bring about reconciliation rather than vengeance. I told Ralph, "It's okay to let Linda know that you don't approve of her actions. Just don't hold in your anger, allowing it to grow into bitterness. We must still communicate love toward a person, even though we are angry at his or her actions or attitudes. Do not express your anger in an uncontrolled manner by yelling and screaming, but through the power of the Holy Spirit, carefully and constructively rebuke her for her sins. The key to this is to make sure you resolve the anger you feel 'before the setting of the sun,' as the apostle Paul tells us in Ephesians 4:26."

Storing unresolved anger is not God's will. Ralph had to learn to forgive Linda's sins immediately so that he would not build up a long list of grievances that would eventually explode into uncontrollable anger. Honest, loving confrontation is far better and more godly than bitterness.

I discussed the third step of learning to use anger constructively in chapter 7: Learn to love your sinning child even though you dislike his or her sin. Ralph's anger did not mean that he did not love his daughter, but rather he was upset at what she was doing to herself and to her parents. Over the weeks that Ralph and I talked about his anger, he began to realize that the emotions caused by parent burnout had compounded his problems with his daughter.

Imagine what the prodigal son's reaction might have been if his father had picked up stones and thrown them at him. He probably would have turned around and gone back to the pig pen! Parents must learn to use their emotions constructively so they will work for God's will rather than against it.

Trust Your Child, But Not Blindly

Ralph and Helen Harrison knew that they must again try to trust Linda, but only if she gave them some indication of her repentance. If a prodigal child repents and seems to accept the parents' faith and values when he or she returns, the parents must not respond to the child with an attitude of cynicism and unbelief. A family might, in fact, celebrate the occasion by enjoying a meal at a good restaurant, just as the father in Jesus' story told his servant to "bring the fatted calf here and kill it, and let us eat and be merry!" (Lk. 15:23).

The father of the prodigal son did not call for the celebration, however, until after the son had said, "Father, I have sinned against heaven and in your sight, and am no longer worthy to be called your son" (Lk. 15:21). The prodigal son was truly repentant.

What if the father had replied to his son's confession by saying, "You can stay in the bunk house with the other servants. If you prove to be a faithful servant in the next year, then I'll acknowledge you as my son"? The son probably would have returned to the pig pen after a few months at home. Parents should never make a child "earn" his place in the family, or their relationship will immediately be threatened. Reconciliation is based on trust and unconditional love.

But not on blind trust. Some prodigals, like Linda, may not have had a change of heart. Linda Harrison had developed a pattern of returning home so she could regain her strength for another madcap adventure. Prodigals, like Linda, just want to be on good terms with the family for social or economic gain. They soon show their unrepentant spirit by using threats to run away again to manipulate their parents. A son or daughter might begin fighting about house rules, such as curfew times. "If you don't allow me to stay out until 2:00 A.M., I'll run away again. It's your fault that I ran away to begin with. I never would have left home if you hadn't been so strict."

ONCE THE PRODIGAL RETURNS

Parents cannot just sigh with relief once the child returns. Instead they must see the prodigal's return as an opportunity to promote right values and beliefs through their words, deeds, and attitudes. Parents must, therefore, continue to invest time and energy to maintain a good relationship with their child and to encourage him or her to grow in his or her understanding of Jesus Christ.

Some prodigals will try to continue their lifestyle of sex or drugs at home. In one case, parents found their nineteen-year-old boy, skinny-dipping in their pool with a sixteen-year-old girl he'd picked up on the strip in Fort Lauderdale. Studies show that most teenagers who are having sexual encounters engage in their acts of sex in their own homes, right after school when both parents are still at work. "Latch-key" prodigals should be encouraged to get involved in supervised afternoon activities at school, or they should be sent to another person's house (a relative or close friend) where they are under adult supervision, or the parents should make special arrangements for them to stay late at school.

Prodigals must understand from the beginning that as long as they live at home, they will have to abide by their parents' rules. If not, they are free to find another place to live. Of course, parents must be willing to be flexible in areas that are simply a matter of taste rather than ethics—clothing, musical styles, the church the prodigal attends. Parents do not want to smother the child's personality or will power; instead they should enable the prodigal to learn to make responsible choices. House rules should include the child's doing basic chores of cleaning and maintenance. Parents should also require that adult prodigals work and contribute to the welfare of the family.

Each prodigal child can again decide to abandon the parents' values. When the Harrisons made it clear to Linda that they would no longer be a part of her "game," she immediately returned to the streets. But the Harrisons have not given up hope. They are still praying that Linda will someday heed God's guiding hand.

THE REPEATING PRODIGAL

What about prodigals like Linda, who seem to habitually leave and return? The Harrisons have made a few stipulations on Linda before allowing her to return home again. Because her addiction to drugs is severe, they will require that she receive extensive help in a rehabilitation center or hospital.

In other cases parents might put the child in a home for delinquent children. Underage prodigals who abuse drugs or alcohol, run away from home for days at a time, are sexually active, or practice violence must agree to regular counseling. The parents' ultimate goal is to provide the most helpful environment for this particular period. Sometimes that isn't home. Regardless of where the prodigal child returns, he or she must know that the parents have accepted him or her back into their hearts, and that their actions are motivated by love.

Unrepentant adult prodigals should be made to face the consequences of their actions. Often these adults return home, as Linda did, and try to get away without paying the price of their behavior. If the child is not really repentant, the parents must be ready to ask the child to leave, especially if his or her actions are disrupting the house or setting a bad example for other children. Parents must also be ready to take an honest look at their parenting strategy to determine if, in some aspect, they are failing to reach their child. Both parents and child should seek the root reasons for this repeating process through professional counseling.

When is Enough, Enough?

Should the parent continue to take the child back, as the Harrisons have done? The guiding principle can be found in Luke 17:3–5 and Matthew 18:21,22. In Matthew's account, Peter asked Jesus, "Lord, how often shall my brother sin against me, and I forgive him? Up to seven times?"

Jesus replied, "I do not say to you, up to seven times, but up to seventy times seven."

In Luke's account, the disciples immediately asked Jesus, "Increase our faith." They, like Peter, thought that forgiving someone seven times was nearly impossible. Parents whose child lives as a prodigal for years have to continually plead with the Lord, "Increase our faith. Help us to make it through one more day, one more week, one more year."

In Matthew's account of Peter's question, Jesus emphasized the importance of the principle of forgiveness by telling the story of a king who wanted to settle accounts with his servants. One servant owed the king 10,000 talents. In today's money this would be worth nearly $45 million, an unheard of amount. Yet when the servant fell on the ground and pleaded, "Master, have patience with me, and I will pay you all," the king forgave him the debt.

We all realize how grateful this servant should have been. Forgive a 45-million-dollar debt? Close to impossible. Yet few of us really feel as grateful to God for forgiving our sins as we should. The price Jesus paid was the agony of the cross, a sacrifice far beyond any monetary sum. It was very costly for God to forgive us; we cannot expect that it will be easy for us to forgive our children. But forgive them, we must.

How did the servant show his gratitude to the king? He immediately went to look for one of his debtors. The man the servant found owed him $7,000—a large sum but infinitely small when compared to the debt he had owed the king. Yet, the servant, who had been forgiven a debt of $45 million, refused to forgive his fellow servant when he pleaded for mercy.

The king could not believe the servant would do such a thing. He quickly chastised him: "Should you not also have had compassion on your fellow servant just as I had pity on you?" The king immediately delivered the servant to the torturers until he could pay his debt.

Jesus did not leave this parable for each disciple's interpretation. He concluded this story, saying, "So My heavenly Father also will do to you if each of you, from his heart, does not forgive his brother his trespasses" (Matt. 18:23–35). Christ left no doubt that we are to forgive each other over and over again. Forgive the sinner, yes. Ignore the sin, no.

Just before Peter asked Jesus the question, "How often shall I forgive my brother?" Jesus had told His disciples how to respond to someone who sinned against them as our prodigal children sin against us. Jesus said, "If your brother sins against you, go and tell him his fault between you and him alone" (Matt. 18:15). Prodigal children must be told that they are sinning.

If the person does not repent of the sin, Jesus advised the disciples, "Take with you one or two more, that by the mouth of two or three witnesses every word may be established" (Matt. 18:16). These "witnesses" could be friends of the family, members of the local church, or other adult members of the family—such as grandparents, aunts, or uncles who have the Christian faith. Their goal should be to discover the truth of the matter, provide objective, third-party insight, and call for repentance of the actual sins. Once this has been accomplished, reconciliation between the parents and the child should be possible.

However, if the child still refuses to repent of his actions, then Jesus said, "Tell it to the church" (Matt. 18:15–19). Call in a Christian counselor, as I have already suggested, or a leader in the church.

Our prodigal children must fully comprehend the pain they have caused *us and God,* each and every time they commit their lives to ungodliness. Even in confrontation, our aim must be to restore them gently, looking for repentance and redemption, not revenge.

PRODIGALS WITH NOWHERE TO GO

Some prodigals have no home to return to, for a number of reasons:

- The breakdown in the relationship with their parents is so great that the parents refuse to have any further interaction with the child
- The parents are dead
- The parents are divorced

- The prodigal's parents are prodigals themselves and do not set a godly example

Whatever the case, the prodigal may come to himself in a far country and find that he has no one to help him. God's answer to these prodigals is, "Believe in Jesus Christ and join My family, the church." The prodigal does have a spiritual family in almost every city and town throughout the world.

A number of prodigals come to the Coral Ridge Presbyterian Church for help, as Sharon did. She became a homeless prodigal when she moved from her family's home in Philadelphia, Pennsylvania, to South Florida at the age of nineteen. Sharon had taken her first drink at the age of eleven and had tried drugs when she was only thirteen. The promise of easy beach living and wild nights lured her to Florida, as it has many other prodigals.

Sharon began hanging around bars on Fort Lauderdale's popular strip and was well on her way to becoming an alcoholic when she started dating a bartender. This gave her even more reason to spend her evenings in the bar, drinking and socializing. Chasing after chemically–induced highs soon became a way of life for her.

One of her friends, who was beginning to question her wild lifestyle, began to attend the outreach meetings at Coral Ridge Presbyterian Chruch and finally convinced Sharon to join her. After this meeting, a member of the outreach group wrote Sharon. "We'll be here if you need help," she said. Sharon didn't respond or attend another meeting, but she did save the letter.

Obviously, our location in Fort Lauderdale makes our outreach ministry particularly important to our church. But I believe that every Christian church should be prepared to reach out in love and compassion to the prodigals in its community. Sharon is one of many young adults who have responded to our program. Often our initial contact seems to have little result, but God uses that contact to reach the young adult at a critical time, as He did with Sharon.

Two months after she attended the meeting, Sharon wandered out of a bar on the strip late at night. She was seeking to sober up, to clear her muddled thinking in the fresh air, so she crossed the street to walk along the beach. Sharon remembered nothing until she woke up on the beach at 3:30 A.M. A man was shaking her. "Would you like a ride home?" he asked.

"I stood up," she later told me, "but I don't remember anything except getting into a car with three guys. They asked me if I knew where a party was." Sharon woke up the next day in her apartment but had no idea how she got there. She'd experienced her first blackout, and that frightened her.

"I knew in my heart there was a void in my life," she said. "I was trying to fill it with drugs and alcohol. Yet, even though I consumed more and more of them, they weren't working.

"I finally admitted that something was really wrong and that I didn't have the answer. Then I remembered the letter and your church. Jesus and the Bible were foreign to me, but I thought the people in that group might be able to help."

Sharon contacted the woman who had written the letter. They talked, and the woman set up an appointment for Sharon with the pastor leading our outreach ministry. During this visit, Sharon accepted Christ as her Savior and Lord. In the next months the members of the group helped her to get a job and to become involved with other church members her own age. Soon she was attending

Sunday services and Bible studies. Jesus' power in her life became so real that she said, "I just lost my desire for drugs and alcohol."

Sharon now actively participates in a counseling ministry in our church. She and homeless prodigals like herself have a spiritual family and a home among God's people. True stories like Sharon's help the Harrisons continue to hope for their own daughter's salvation. They are willing to forgive Linda "seventy times seven" so that one day she, too, will come home.

10

What If My Prodigal Never Comes Home?

Fran and Ted Spyak's only worry about their daughter, Carol, was that she was too much of an idealist. She always tried to live her Christian beliefs and expected everyone else to do so, too. During her years in junior high school she became an officer of the Christian Youth Fellowship at her church, attended Bible studies, and tried to witness to her friends at school.

Carol began to be disillusioned with Christianity during her high school years, however. At dinner one Sunday she complained to her mother and father, "How can the church spend thousands of dollars on a parking lot when people are starving throughout the world? Jesus said we were to love one another. Yet our church seems more interested in money and buildings."

"Some adults also resisted spending money on a new parking lot, Carol," Fran Spyak said. "But where would we meet without a church building and where would we park our cars without a parking lot? Sometimes we might overemphasize these things, but believe me," Fran assured her daughter, "our church is interested in helping others. At Christmas we prepare baskets of food for the shut-ins."

"Big deal! That's only once a year, Mom. What about the people who need help all year long?"

Carol paused a minute to see if her mother had an

answer. Then she proceeded to voice her second gripe. "Do you know what happened last week at youth meeting? That old Mr. Tyler told us not to play our guitars so loud during our meetings. 'It's not right to make so much noise in the church,' he said.

"All we were doing was singing some contemporary Christian songs. Doesn't he understand that we won't come to church if it's dull and boring?"

Ted and Fran Spyak liked Mr. Tyler despite his crusty disposition, so they tried to help Carol understand that the man meant well. "Mr. Tyler associates guitars with rock and roll, and he believes that music is sinful and worldly," Ted Spyak said. "You need to understand how he is."

Carol just shook her head in disgust. "If Christians can't accept one another and don't live what they believe, what is Christianity all about anyway?"

A few Sundays later Carol told her parents that she had been successful in getting a friend from school, Michelle Morris, to go to church with her. The Spyaks were pleased until the two girls walked into the sanctuary. Carol had not told her parents that Michelle was black. Even though Carol attended a school that was a third black and Hispanic, the Spyaks attended a church in a nearby wealthy suburb. Michelle was the first black to ever enter the church.

The morning went well for Carol and Michelle. Although most of the young people attended the local school, George Jepsen, a popular leader in the youth group, was a classmate of Carol and Michelle. Michelle felt at home in the service and Sunday school, and George talked and joked with the girls after church. As Michelle got out of the car she said she would like to attend services next week.

Carol was pleased. She did not suspect that others

might feel differently. At the conclusion of the evening service that night, Pastor Burner asked Carol to come to his office. After a few cursory questions about her family, he asked, "So Carol, you brought a friend today. What was her name?"

Carol was a bit nervous. The pastor had never asked to speak with her in his office before. "Uh . . . Michelle. She's a friend from school and a great person," she answered as if to justify her actions. "Michelle really liked our church. She wants to come back next week."

"Why doesn't she go to her family's church?" Pastor Burner asked

"Her parents don't go to church. Never have. Why do you want to know?" Carol wondered out loud.

"Well, if you tell me where she lives, I can probably suggest a church closer to her neighborhood."

"Michelle doesn't want to go to a church where she doesn't know anyone. She knows George and me and likes the services here. Why send her to another church?"

Pastor Burner moved his chair forward and looked straight at Carol. "Your friend's presence in church upset a number of our people. Don't you think she would be happier in a church with 'her own kind'?"

"I-I-I can't believe you said that. You're just as bad as . . ." Carol stopped herself in mid-sentence. She stood up immediately. "Don't worry," she assured Pastor Burner, "Michelle will not be back, because I'm never coming back!"

Pastor Burner started to protest, "I didn't mean . . ." but Carol walked out of the office before she heard anymore. Later, as she raced her car toward home, tears rolled down her face. One word kept pounding in her mind PREJU-DICE . . . PREJUDICE . . . He's supposed to be a man of God, a pastor, yet he's more prejudiced than anyone at our school.

Carol told her parents about the incident as soon as she got home. "I'll never go back to that church. Never! All the 'Do unto others' pastor preaches . . . it's all a lie!"

Carol kept her word. To her parents' surprise, she never returned. Ted Spyak asked Pastor Burner to talk to her, to apologize, but he refused. "Carol's the one who should apologize," he maintained.

When Carol's friends at church found out why she had left, George Jepsen and ten other kids also walked out. Two months later, the youth director resigned. Still many of the church members saw the entire episode as the inevitable result of having too large a youth ministry which reached out to too many other neighborhoods.

Finally, Ted and Fran Spyak looked for another church. They could not believe that their pastor had refused to apologize to Carol. A small church just down the street from their house seemed to have a warmer atmosphere. They even thought Carol might attend, since black and white Christians worshiped together there. Still Carol refused to attend. "I've had enough of church for a while," she insisted.

As the months went by, Ted and Fran began to notice that Carol's friends shifted from the kids in the old youth group and her friends from high school to young people who looked as if they were on drugs. When the Spyaks questioned Carol about her friends, she assured them, "Oh, they have a few problems, but they are really good kids." Ted and Fran did not feel they could question her any further since she obeyed the rules of the house. She has the right to select her own friends since she is now seventeen, they thought.

Once Carol graduated from high school, she moved into her own apartment and attended a junior college. There she met people who were involved in eastern philosophy and studied some of the ideas of Buddhism and Hinduism.

Carol never adopted these philosophies but she occasionally took a portion of their thinking and used it to justify her actions. When she lost her job because she consistently failed to show up on time, Carol told her parents, "Well, it's just because of bad Karma. You can't escape such things. You have to pay your dues from past lives."

Carol soon began to drink socially and became sexually active. The Spyaks learned of her new lifestyle from one of their close friends whose daughter had known Carol in high school. They decided not to confront her but to work to reestablish lines of communication with her and to continue to show their love and support. They hoped that Carol would work through this stage and return to her Christian beliefs and values.

Then one afternoon in Carol's sophomore year in college, Fran answered the phone to hear a male voice ask, "Is this Carol Spyak's mother?"

"Yes," Fran replied quickly. "Is something wrong?"

"Ma'am, this is Officer Cahill. I am sorry to tell you this, but your daughter has been hit by a car. Would you and your husband please come to the Southridge Hospital emergency ward as soon as possible?"

When the Spyaks arrived at the hospital, the officer told them that Carol had been crossing a street near her apartment when the automobile struck her. "The doctors could not save her," the officer said softly. "I'm afraid your daughter's dead."

Unfortunately, too many prodigals die before they seem to return to Christianity or its ethical values. Sometimes death is caused by the prodigal's own lifestyle, as a result of drugs or suicide, and other times, the death is the result of an illness or accident.

Some parents in this situation become bitter and turn against God and His truth. They themselves become prodigals.

Facing a Prodigal's Death

A parent in the Bible faced this same situation, and the tragedies that happened to him go way beyond the three difficulties many people anticipate when they say, "Bad luck always comes in threes."

One day Job was a wealthy, happy father, whose riches were counted by the thousands of sheep, camels, and cattle he possessed. The next day, Job should have remained in bed, as the old saying goes. In a matter of hours all his herds were destroyed and his children killed by a great wind—Hurricane Uz, you might say—which struck the house where his children were celebrating their elder brother's birthday.

Not one child, not two, but all ten of Job's children were killed in one gigantic quirk of nature, phenomena that Job knew were ultimately from the hand of his God who ruled the heavens and the earth. How did Job respond?

He tore his robe, shaved his head—the ancient signs of mourning—and fell to the ground. In a swoon of self-pity? No, to worship the Living God. "Naked I came from my mother's womb, and naked shall I return there," Job cried out. "The LORD gave, and the LORD has taken away; Blessed be the name of the LORD" (Job 1:21).

At this point many would think that Job would have become a prodigal. Many would justify Job for turning against God. Most of us in Job's position would have cried out to God, "You are a mean and capricious God who loves to watch His people suffer. I shall never trust you again. I shall not follow your ways. I'm done. Finished! Through!"

But Job resisted this temptation, even though he did not understand what was happening to him. He didn't know, as we do, that his disasters were part of the battle in the "heavenlies" between God and Satan (see Eph. 6:10–18). Satan had questioned Job's love of God and allegiance to

Him. The devil had asked God, "Have You not made a hedge around him?" "Stretch out Your hand and touch all that he has . . ." Satan challenged God. "Surely he will curse You to your face!"

God in his infinite wisdom, power, and love allowed Satan to tempt Job. "Only do not lay a hand on his person," God had told Satan. It is important to note here that Satan is under the sovereign rule of God and could not have afflicted Job without the Almighty's permission.

In the first test, Satan's boast of weakness of Job's faith was shown to be a horrible lie. God was glorified through Job's faith. The devil returned to heaven defeated.

God again pointed out to Satan the virtue of Job and how he had passed the test. Satan now made a new accusation. Not wanting to be shown before the whole court of heaven to have been wrong, he proclaimed "A man will give up anything to save his life." Then he again challenged God. "Touch his body with sickness and he will curse you to your face!"

"He is in your power," God answered, "but spare his life." (Job 2:1–6). Again God accepted Satan's challenge and for His own wise and good purposes allowed the devil to do his evil deeds. Note that God never did any evil but only allowed Satan to take the actions of his own rebellious and darkened heart.

Soon Job's body was covered with boils—festering, pus–filled, bleeding, stinging sores. (Some scholars think this may have been leprosy.)[1] One can picture Job looking much like a leper or third-degree burn patient, his features distorted beyond recognition and the pain from his infected skin interfering with any of his normal activities.

His wife's faith cracked under this pressure. She had seen the death of her children, the loss of all their worldly possessions, and now the ruination of her husband's health. She cried out to her husband, her voice filled with anger at God and pity for herself and Job. "Curse God and die!" (Job 2:9).

Some of us would have taken this advice. Some who suffer consider suicide or fall into depression filled with bitter hatred for God and life. Instead, Job admonished his wife, "You speak as one of the foolish women speaks. Shall we indeed accept good from God, and shall we not accept adversity?" (Job 2:10). Again Satan's ploy had been defeated and God's name glorified.

However, God's plan was not just to defeat Satan. He also had allowed this tragedy to take place for the good of Job. While Job initially responded to his suffering with faith, as his suffering continued without relief, he, like us, finally began to wonder about the value of living a good life. Was God treating him justly?

After all, the Bible says that Job was "blameless and upright . . . one who feared God and shunned evil" (Job 1:1). He also was a good parent. We know that he cared for the religious training of his ten children, since he prayed for them regularly. The Bible says that after the annual feasts to celebrate his children's birthdays, Job would rise early in the morning and offer burnt offerings for them. "It may be," he said, "that my sons have sinned and cursed God in their hearts" (Job 1:5). Perhaps Job was worried that his children were becoming prodigals since their parties could have resulted in drunkenness and ungodliness.

Slowly Job began to doubt God. "Why, God?" he now asked, as we all do. "Why have you taken everything from me? If you love me, if you have appreciated my love for you, why would you do such a thing?"

Job began to be filled with righteous pride. He reminded his friends and God of the sins he could have committed, but didn't. I could "have longed for another man's wife. . . ." I could "have been unfair to my servants. . . ." I could "have put my trust in money. . . ." (See Job 31:9–40, TLB.) If I'd done any of these things, Job was saying, I might understand what has happened to me. But I haven't!

Once Job gave in to the sin of righteous pride, his image of God changed. Now he saw God as a capricious master, rather than a just, loving father: "He [God] leads counselers away plundered, And makes fools of judges. . . . He makes nations great, and destroys them" (Job 12:17–23).

Finally, in a fit of righteous indignation, Job cried out, "Oh, that the Almighty would answer me, . . . I would declare to Him the number of my steps; Like a prince I would approach Him" (Job 31:35,37).

Job felt so sure of his own righteousness that he wanted a private conference with God, in which he knew he would be vindicated and God's actions seen as wrong. Job sinned because he doubted God's righteousness, instead of realizing that perhaps God's actions were right when one had all the facts about the universe, God's plan, and Job's heart.

At that moment, Job was close to becoming a prodigal. His questioning of God could have hardened into a grudge against God, a bitterness that would have kept Job away from God. The longer Job ignored God, the more the grudge would have grown, finally exploding into hatred and unbelief.

Yet Job avoided this error. Though he battled with doubt and despair, he still uttered the greatest words of faith ever recorded: "I know that my Redeemer lives, And he shall stand at last on the earth" (Job 19:25).

Many of us hear Handel's beautiful rendition of these words, in the middle of his great oratio *The Messiah,* and associate this affirmation of faith with the beauty and glory of life. We hear trumpets sounding and angels singing. We see the heavens opening up and the glory of God sitting on His throne surrounded by His angels.

Yet Job didn't see this glorious sight when he said those words. He said them when he was feeling just as parents feel when their prodigals die—deserted, broken, ashamed—wondering why God allows such tragedy to happen to them.

How did Job maintain his faith in spite of his pain and loss?

THREE PRINCIPLES

Let's examine what happened to Job so we can identify the principles that kept him from rejecting God.

1. Belief in God and life after death

In suffering, as in success, the most important part of Job's life was his relationship with God and the opportunity to meet Him face-to-face and live with Him forever. This commitment kept pulling him away from suicide and despair to seek God. Job told his friends, "And after my skin is destroyed, this I know, That in my flesh I shall see God . . . I shall see for myself . . . How my heart yearns within me!" (Job 19:26–27).

2. A Counselor

Even though Job's faith held him fairly steady, he still might have faltered if God had not sent a godly counselor, Elihu, the fourth friend who came to visit him. Unlike Job's other counselors, Elihu did not accuse Job of having a secret sin which only God knew about. Instead, Elihu pointed out to Job his real sin.

"Look, in this you are not righteous. I will answer you; For God is greater than man. Why do you contend with Him? For He does not give an accounting of any of His words." (Job 33:12–13).

Job was so sure he would win his case in a fair trial before the Almighty. Anyone who made such a statement,

Elihu said, had ceased being the submissive servant of God, the great King.

Elihu acted as a good friend. He urged Job to trust God as a perfectly wise, perfectly good, divine teacher who was using Job's afflictions to teach him godliness. Elihu's counsel implied that even the loss of Job's children was part of God's plan. It helped Job find the intellectual answers to the dilemma that filled his brain and agonized his soul.

But the agony of Job's soul could not be healed merely by hearing the right message about God, just as our agony cannot be healed without encountering the presence of God Himself.

3. God's presence and direct answer

Elihu's counsel had prepared the ground for Job to encounter God Himself. God answered Job directly by manifesting Himself in a massive storm. He reminded Job, "Where were you when I laid the foundations of the earth? Tell me, if you have understanding" (Job 38:4).

After experiencing the presence of God in the storm, Job answered, "I have heard of You by the hearing of the ear, But now my eye sees You. Therefore I abhor myself, and repent in dust and ashes" (Job 42:5-6).

God's presence was able to bring peace to Job's heart. He took back his accusations about God and repented of his self-righteousness. Faith is born and maintained in us ultimately not by an act of our wills but through God Himself encountering us and changing our hearts.

It is the same today in our lives as God sometimes touches us in a supernatural way. We feel His touch deep inside as we struggle with the agonies and issues of our lives. This direct encounter will change us as it changed Job.

God used the tremendous afflictions that Satan put

upon Job to strengthen Job's faith, not weaken it. He removed Job's tendency toward pride and self-righteousness. He can do the same for us.

Parents who experience the death of their prodigal children must look to these three elements—a firm faith, a godly counselor, and the encounter of God's presence—as the elements will deliver them from despair to a greater faith.

Job did not know the future, any more than we do. He did not know that God would bless his later life, even more than his beginning. No storybook has a happier ending than this story of Job's affliction. God doubled Job's herds: the seven thousand sheep were replaced by fourteen thousand, the three thousand camels with six thousand. God gave Job 140 years of life and ten more children—seven sons and three daughters.

As we face the loss of our prodigal children we must accept it as part of God's plan. Through this agony God may give us a deeper understanding of Himself, which will lead to greater peace and happiness. Or He may give us a greater compassion for others who suffer. The one fact we can be sure of is that He is working all the events of our life together for good and not evil.

When Ted and Fran Spyak came to me for spiritual counseling after Carol's death, I reminded them of Job's trials and how he endured. Then I pointed out four spiritual realities which are crucial to overcoming such pain. These realities can provide a solid anchor for our souls in any crisis.

SPIRITUAL REALITY ONE: GOD IS STILL IN CONTROL

Sometimes, as in Carol's fatal accident, our prodigal child's death is caused by someone's sinful acts. When this happens, the person, like the driver of that car, is guilty of a crime. Yet, even in such cases, God is still in control. The sin of man is not greater than the sovereign will of God.

Men sin, but God uses such sin to accomplish his plans. The Scriptures clearly teach that "it is appointed for men to die once" (Heb. 9:27) and that the time of death is determined before we are born (see Ps. 139:16).

The Spyaks had to be willing to admit that Carol's death was no mere "accident of fate," "bad luck," or "raw deal," but was under the control of God. Then their endless questions of "What if?" and "If only?" could be forgotten as they accepted that in a fallen world there is indeed a God-ordained time to live and a time to die (Eccles. 3:1–8). Once they accepted this truth, they were able to surrender their wills to God's higher wisdom and trust in His perfect judgement.

We know that, as in Job's case, God can use this difficult experience, which is not good in itself, for our good. Paul assured that:

> . . . we know that all things work together for good to those who love God, to those who are the called according to His purpose. For whom He foreknew, He also predestined to be conformed to the image of His Son, that He might be the firstborn among many brethren. (Rom. 8:28–29)

Every experience of temporal suffering and pain is used by God to make us more like Jesus. Jesus had to remain true to God's will as He faced the necessity of going through the painful suffering of the cross, and we must do so too, when we face our own personal trials and griefs. Without suffering, we could not become like Him.

SPIRITUAL REALITY TWO: WE DO NOT KNOW

Whereas the death of any child is hard for parents to accept, the death of a prodigal child is doubly hard. Most parents have viewed their child as lost, and they have longed for the time when he or she will come to a true saving faith.

But now the child is dead, and the parents feel that he or she is eternally lost. How can they face the horrible knowledge that their beloved child is now suffering the fires of the eternal hell? These thoughts had driven the Spyaks to a depth of sorrow, which seemed to be beyond comfort.

"However, you do not know that Carol is lost," I reminded them. "You may think she is, but no one has absolute knowledge, since we do not know the full circumstances of Carol's life.

"Carol may have been saved even though you did not know it. The inner battles of someone's heart may not be immediately manifested in either a public confession of faith or a change of lifestyle. Yet inwardly the person has begun to believe in Jesus as Lord and Savior. Since you don't know the exact disposition of Carol's heart when she died, you must not jump to the conclusion that she is lost. Doing so," I warned them "is to assume the role of God, who alone is the final judge."

Fran Spyak began to cry as I was telling them this spiritual reality. When I finished, she exclaimed, "Oh, Dr. Kennedy, that's exactly why I have been so upset. I felt that Carol was just beginning to turn around. And then she died . . . maybe she did make a commitment that we knew nothing about."

Fran then told me about a Sunday Carol had spent with her parents about five months before her death. After dinner Carol had said, "I really love you, Mom and Dad. When you first found out about my drinking and messing around, I figured you would hate me and disown me."

"But you have stood by me, even though you believe I am headed down the wrong road. I wish more Christians were like you. Perhaps I would come back to the church." Carol had gotten up from the table and come to hug each of her parents.

"Don't worry," she said as she had helped them clear the table, "one day I'll get my head together . . . You'll see."

"Carol was so like a little child that day," Fran Spyak told me. "So confused, so hurt, yet for the first time I saw hope."

"And in the next months she came to church with us each Sunday and even attended some special functions. She seemed to like our pastor and went to see him a few times on her own. Maybe she did have a change of heart . . ." Fran Spyak looked at me, as if asking for confirmation of her statement.

"None of us can know that now . . . It is even impossible to say what happened in those last seconds just before she died. If a person cries out to Jesus in true faith at that time, he or she is saved. No one knows this except for Jesus and the person."

How often I have had to remind parents of this spiritual truth: No one knows. In fact, the entire Christian church must remember this sober fact. We are *not* the final judge. We cannot say that a particular person is suffering the agonies of hell. Parents should not fear that their offspring will be treated unfairly or harshly at the judgment, for the Lord is the very foundation of justice, and His mercy is without end.

SPIRITUAL REALITY THREE: YOU MUST LOVE ME MORE THAN THESE

The present-day church has been far too quiet about the radical loyalty Jesus requires of His followers. Jesus clearly states that our relationship to Him must come before all others. When He was instructing His disciples, He warned them, "He who loves father or mother more

169

than Me is not worthy of Me. And he who loves son or daughter more than Me is not worthy of Me. And he who does not take his cross and follow after Me is not worthy of Me" (Matt. 10:37–38).

Jesus knew that faith in Him could become a point of contention in homes and bring about division in the family relationship. He told His disciples, "I did not come to bring peace but a sword. For I have come to 'set a man against his father, a daughter against her mother, and a daughter-in-law against her mother-in-law.' And a man's foes will be those of his own household" (Matt. 10:34–36).

Jesus clearly understood the natural ties of the family might be strained to the breaking point because of a person's radical faith in Him. Yet He refused to play second fiddle to our family loyalties.

Parents who have lost a prodigal child must not turn against Christ because their child is dead. To do so would be to side with the child in his sinful actions against Jesus and to fail to love the Lord as they should. If Jesus condemns our child to hell for his sins, we still must love Him enough to stand in agreement with Him in this judgment.

As I point out this call to absolute and ultimate loyalty to Jesus Christ, it is important to remember that He loves to see entire families worship Him together (Ps. 22:27). Yet, in our fallen world, this does not always happen. While Jesus takes no pleasure or delight in the death and judgment of the wicked, He must execute judgment as the holy King of the Universe.

SPIRITUAL REALITY FOUR: THE GOD OF ALL COMFORT

Our God is well acquainted with grief. His heart was broken when men became consumed by acts of violence and sexual immorality after the fall. (See Gen. 6.) Jesus cried over the city of Jerusalem when the people refused to repent. And it is impossible for us to imagine God's sorrow as He watched His Son die a slow, painful, humiliating death on the cross for our sins.

God even knows the sorrow of having a prodigal child who never comes home. Each person who goes to hell was created by God in His own image. Parents must remember that their prodigal children were not theirs alone, but God's, too.

Since God understands your grief, He is able to meet your sorrow, share your tears, and bring comfort into your shattered lives if you will spend time with Him in prayer and Bible reading. It's no coincidence that quotations from the book of Psalms are used on greeting cards to express love and concern. Many people have been able to avoid sleepless nights of anguish by reading the Psalms before they go to bed. Often God will send parents who have gone through similar suffering to share their compassion and love with you.

MY CHILD IS ALIVE, BUT I HAVE NO HOPE

Some parents of living prodigals experience many of the same spiritual problems and crises as those parents whose children have died. These prodigal children are so deeply committed to non-Christian beliefs and behavior that their parents have given up hope that they will ever change. Once hope is gone, they are plagued with depression, just as parents who have been told their child is dead.

While the spiritual realities for grieving parents may be of some help, such parents should remember a basic fact: *As long as there is life, there is usually hope.* No one is beyond the redeeming blood of Christ. To give up on a prodigal child is to give up on the power of the gospel of Christ to save.

The core of Christianity teaches that those who are sinners—dead in transgressions, opposed to the purposes

of God and dedicated to evil—can be transformed by the
Holy Spirit and the Word. To stop believing this is to
become dominated by a spirit of doubt and unbelief in the
power of God to redeem.

Parents must recognize such feelings are sinful and
remind themselves of the grace and power of our Lord
Jesus Christ. Facing the prodigal process in unbelief will
always lead to despair; facing it in faith will supply a
positive influence on our children and fill our lives with
hope.

11

Will My Other Children Become Prodigals?

Dear Dad,

I will never be able to forgive Produs, so I refuse to be a part of any welcome home party for him. It is hard for me to understand why you would allow this sinner back after all he has done. I always thought that you preferred him to me. This just proves it. Even though I have always been a loyal son, you have never done anything special for me or my friends.

Sincerely,
Judd

Henry Atkinson, one of the most popular boys in the local high school, was a gifted guitar player, and athlete. For years his younger brothers, John and Jim had looked up to him. Who wouldn't want to follow in his footsteps?

Henry was so talented as an athlete that he was the star of the football team in his junior year. Every ball the quarterback threw in Henry's direction landed firmly in his grip, and he could usually convert a good catch into a

173

substantial gain because he was so fast and able to dodge the opposition. Once football season was over Henry turned his talents to the stage and became the star of the school musical.

The attention Henry received from the girls in the senior class as well as his own class was so tempting that he soon decided to enjoy the fruits of his popularity. He and his best friend began a contest to see who could go to bed with the most girls in a week.

Henry used his upbeat personality to lure girls at school and even some he met at parties, many of whom were on drugs. They convinced him to try marijuana and other drugs. These girls so willingly complied with his desires that they soon became uninteresting to Henry. Instead, he sought to overcome the resistance of the girls in his youth group. Life was a game to Henry, and sex was just another competitive sport. As always, he had to win.

John, who was two years younger than Henry, soon decided to try to mimic Henry's athletic and sexual prowess. Henry willingly introduced John to marijuana and told him some easy ways to lie to their dad so he wouldn't be caught. Henry and John double-dated a few times, and at Henry's suggestion they competed to see who could get his date to go all the way first.

Jim, who was four years younger than Henry, watched his brothers' actions. He knew he could probably never compete with their popularity since he tended to be a loner. Slowly he began to resent them.

One Friday evening when Henry's father was supposed to be working late and his brothers were attending a school basketball game, Henry invited one of his girlfriends to the house. For the first time, Henry got caught by his father, who decided to come home early because he was exhausted. Embarrassed and angry, Ted Atkinson ordered both of the teenagers to get dressed. He asked the girl to leave and then confronted Henry.

By then Henry had regained his composure. He just smiled and said, "Dad, it's nothing I haven't done before. I'm a man now. I have my needs and there are plenty of girls who'll meet them. I'm sure you did the same things when you were young."

Ted looked at his son in disbelief. Six years ago, when his wife had left him for another man, Ted Atkinson had known that raising three boys by himself would not be easy. Now he realized that he had been so proud of his oldest son's successes and so busy working sixty hours a week, he'd never seen how Henry had changed.

"I don't agree, Henry. I think this is serious. I'm going to make an appointment with a Christian counselor, and we're going to talk about this with him."

"Hey, wait a minute, Dad. I'm not crazy. Why do I need a counselor? I can get any girl I want. I've been offered three scholarships to college. I couldn't be happier. If anyone has a problem, you do!"

The argument didn't end until Ted sent Henry to his room. When John and Jim returned later that night, they knew something was wrong because their dad was still up.

Ted Atkinson decided to go to work late the next day so he could talk to Henry. He went to Henry's room and knocked on the door. There was no answer. Ted opened the door and immediately saw an open window and an empty room. Henry had run away.

Ted called the office and told them he would not be at work that day because of a personal crisis. Then he suggested that the younger boys stay home from school so they could talk about their problems.

Ted began by asking the boys how much they knew about Henry's activities. At first, they shrugged their shoulders, but gradually Ted learned the extent of Henry's involvement with sex and drugs. In the next days he also discovered that John was beginning to get involved in the same lifestyle.

This tendency for the younger children in a family to adopt the older child's bad habits is common. Like Ted, many parents have to take steps to help their younger children at the same time that they are trying to reach the runaway. The siblings are as much a part of the prodigal child syndrome as the parents and the prodigal child himself. Often the younger siblings' responses to the prodigal's behavior give the parents a clue as to how to meet their children's individual needs.

FIRST RESPONSE: REJECTION

Some siblings reject the prodigal, just as the elder brother did in Jesus' parable. This reaction, which might at first seem to be a healthy one, is much more dangerous than parents might think.

In the parable, the elder brother showed his rejection by refusing to join the party. "Lo, these many years I have been serving you," he reminded his father. "I never transgressed your commandment at any time, and yet you never gave me a young goat that I might make merry with my friends.

"But as soon as this son of yours came, who has devoured your livelihood with harlots, you killed the fatted calf for him" (see Luke 15:29–30).

The elder brother was overcome by the sins of jealousy and self-righteousness. Obviously, the elder brother's claim that he never disobeyed any command given by his father was not true. No child is that good! As the eldest, he knew he would receive two-thirds of his father's goods, whereas the prodigal son only received one-third. He had no reason to be so jealous.

Pride is one of the hardest sins to detect. Many outwardly moral people suffer from this transgression of the heart. In this parable the elder brother represented the Pharisees of Jesus' time—people Jesus denounced, calling them "serpents" and "brood of vipers." After mentioning a list of their sins that runs on for twenty verses of Matthew 23, Jesus asked them, "How can you escape the condemnation of hell?"

At the end of the story of the prodigal son, the elder brother is the prodigal, not the younger son. He is unrepentant and wallowing in the sins of self-pity and jealousy. The elder brother is standing outside of God's kingdom, lost and needing to be found.

Siblings who have fallen into the trap of the Pharisees will reject the prodigal because they are moralistic and self-righteous. They see the Christian faith as a moralistic religion, rather than a lifestyle based on God's mercy and forgiveness. They are quick to judge the failures of other members of the family yet blind to their own faults.

Other siblings may reject the prodigal because of sibling rivalry. Now that their brother or sister has openly rejected the values of the home, the siblings seize this opportunity to get the parents' attention and approval by contrasting their own obedience with the prodigal's disobedience. By doing this they think they have finally won the competition and have gained the most favored status.

Ted Atkinson's youngest son, Jim, reacted in this manner. He had always felt inferior to his popular brothers. When Henry ran away, Jim, though at first hesitant, eventually denounced him as "not caring about the rest of us" and told his father everything he knew about what Henry and John were doing. He even made up a few incidents.

Parents have to be careful not to encourage this behavior. Often we are inclined to like the feedback we get from these children, since we feel hurt and rejected by the prodigal and may need another child to side with "us" against "him." We are tempted to reinforce the brother's or sister's reaction, rather than to recognize it as a dangerous, sinful response.

Parents need to lovingly confront siblings who reject the prodigal by reminding them that God saved us by grace and, therefore, wants us to forgive others. They might read Matthew 18, which I discussed in Chapter 9, with their children and help them to see the meaning of Jesus' words, "So My heavenly Father also will do to you if each of you, from his heart, does not forgive his brother his trespasses" (Matt. 18:35).

One important aspect of the prodigal story needs to be brought out at this point. Although it is a happy tale, which points to the redemption of a son who has been lost in a life of wild living, it is also a sad account of how a father still lost a son because of the son's self-righteousness and pride. We need to remember this, and it should humble us to know that, in the end, the son who stayed a prodigal was the self-righteous sibling who never acted out his rebellious attitudes.

This indicates that no pat answers will prevent a child from becoming a prodigal. While we may be inclined to blame the problems of the elder brother on his younger brother, this would not be right. The elder brother chose to respond sinfully to his father's love and his brother's reconciliation.

SECOND RESPONSE: REINFORCEMENT

Parents often find that siblings copy the prodigal's destructive behavior, as John Atkinson did. John maintained that his father had been too hard on Henry. "You've had your head in the sand," John told his dad, "ever since Mom left. You're always working overtime so we never see you. Now you're suddenly concerned about what we've been doing. It's too late to change that, Dad."

Most often the sibling who stands up for the prodigal is romanticizing the prodigal's actions and imitating his way of life. I call this "sibling peer pressure." Children within the same family often form their own social group, and the eldest (or older) son or daughter naturally becomes the leader. The older child also becomes the siblings' primary role model, so the younger children are more interested in pleasing this older brother or sister than in pleasing the parents.

Sometimes, however, reinforcement, like rejection, can stem from sibling rivalry. The other children see that the prodigal gets a great deal of attention, and they wrongly assume that they can get the same attention if they become like him.

Unfortunately, one prodigal child can sometimes set off a prodigal chain reaction, in which hidden opposition to the rules and values of the parents suddenly erupts from several children. Sometimes these children may be secret prodigals, who never openly departed from the family values yet disagreed with them. This chain reaction must be stopped quickly.

HOW TO STOP THIS DANGEROUS CHAIN REACTION

Step One: Reopen Communication and Reestablish Your Position as a Role Model

The first step in this process is to reestablish the lines of communication with the children who are reinforcing the prodigal's actions. This should begin with a family meeting in which the actions of the prodigal child are discussed openly. It should be made clear that the rebellious sibling is still loved but that his actions are self-destructive. The other children also need to understand that their lives will be hurt if they follow his path.

Parents must guard against allowing their time and energy to be totally consumed with the prodigal.

They can effectively model the right behavior for those children who are still in the home more readily than for the prodigal who has left in an act of rebellion.

Ted Atkinson naturally was worried about both his sons' reactions to Henry's prodigal behavior. John was becoming a prodigal and Jim was obviously turning against his brother. Leaders in our church warned Ted that he must avoid the tendency to concentrate his efforts on Henry, which would further damage his relationship with the younger boys.

Step Two: Reevaluate Your Parenting Strategy

Once the prodigal process has begun to spread to another child in the family, parents who at first ignored their own problems may be shocked into taking a more realistic look at the situation.

Homes Without a Previous Parenting Strategy

Ted Atkinson had never really developed a parenting strategy. He needed to take a careful look at how he was running the home to see if John's accusations were partially true. The check list on the opposite page will help parents to evaluate the relationship within their home.

As Ted Atkinson answered these questions, he realized that he had always feared that his wife's promiscuous lifestyle would set a sexual standard for her sons. After all, if Mom ran around on Dad, why can't we fool around? Researchers Robert Coles and Geoffrey Stokes found that kids from divorced families are about twice as likely to engage in premarital sex than those whose parents are still together. According to studies by Coles and Stokes,

PARENTING CHECK LIST

1. Have we been involved in an unbiblical practice?

2. Are we failing to consider our children as a high priority in our lives?

3. Do we spend more time involved in other activities—work, social events—than we do with our family?

4. Is most of our communication with our children negative—injunctions shouted out quickly, in the midst of a busy pace that never stops?

5. Have we resorted to using spanking or physical punishment as an answer to every problem, rather than spending time teaching our children in a positive manner why they should follow Christian beliefs and practice?

6. Have we created unrealistic rules? Too early curfews? Too many dating restrictions?

7. Have we been too lax, which indicates to our children that we don't care how they act?

8. Is there any plan or strategy to our parenting, or is it made up of unconsidered responses to whatever crisis arises?

9. When we are wrong, do we admit this to our children?

10. Do we have a fear—loss of a job, loss of a mate from divorce or death—which we hide even from ourselves, which keeps us from assuming parental responsibilities that would help to stop the prodigal process?

marital status also correlates to how much attention children pay to a parent's views on sex. Thirty-eight percent of the children of married parents say their parents' attitudes affect sexual behavior. Only 20 percent of the kids from divorced parents say the same.[1]

Ted now wished that he and the boys had gone to a counselor after his wife left home. He contacted a Christian counselor associated with our church, and he and his younger sons began a series of weekly meetings with a counselor. He also made changes in other areas, which I will discuss later in this chapter.

Homes with a Parenting Strategy

Even in homes where a parenting strategy has been established, it would be wise to purposely change some of the ways you are approaching your children. Many times children know your patterns and what to expect and they have built defenses around themselves based on this knowledge.

Restructuring your parenting strategy could include:

- Finding new ways to express unconditional love
- Reminding yourself of your God-given authority
- Calling on help from other Christian leaders and family
- Applying consistent discipline
- Allotting more time to be intimate with your children
- Changing the way you relate to your children

Since you have already developed a parenting strategy, you may wonder, *What can I do differently?* How can I change the way I relate to my children?

Each family will be different. Maybe it will mean going on more family weekend outings. Or, if you have had a tendency to be harsh in non-vital areas such as dress codes, loosen up. While in vital areas like curfews, dating, and substance abuse, tighten up. If your children expect you to come home, eat dinner, and spend the night in front of the television, change this pattern. Break out a family game, like Monopoly, and spend the evening playing the game with them. Do the unexpected, attempting to show your love, your desire to know them, and your authority in the home.

By conducting an honest self-examination, correcting any deficiencies in the structure of the home, and changing our strategy, parents may bring about reconciliation with the prodigal and the other children.

Relationship with the Prodigal

Ted Atkinson's relationship with Henry became progressively worse. Henry had found refuge at his best friend's house, a teen who had dropped out of high school and whose parents allowed him to do anything he wished. Part of Ted's parenting strategy for Henry was to change the locks on the doors and to inform Henry that he could only return if he was willing to get counseling for his drug use and sexual behavior.

While our obedient children are enjoying the blessings of the covenant, our beginning prodigals must be consistently punished for their misbehavior. They must also come to understand that their problems are their own doing—not caused by us, or by other brothers or sisters who are having problems in their lives.

Children must be told to face the fact that they alone will bear the responsibility, punishment, and consequences of their own actions. While assuring them we will always be here to help, they must understand we will not tolerate their irresponsible behavior.

Parents must express genuine concern, but also clearly explain to the prodigal that he or she will not receive special attention because of his or her actions. While being willing to help a return to the proper path, parents must communicate that wrong actions lead to bad consequences, and that they will not "bail out" their children from problems created by their irresponsible behavior.

Ted notified the high school of his son's behavior and new living arrangements so that they could monitor his behavior. Henry soon found out that his popularity with the staff at school declined, many of his friends began to spend less time with him, and a local college which had offered him a scholarship withdrew its offer. Henry was beginning to see that irresponsible living could have negative effects.

Step Three: Hedges To Keep the Prodigal Process From Spreading

Our parenting strategy must build hedges around our other children so the prodigal process can be stopped.

1. The Establishment of Solid Rules

The first hedge to consider is the establishment of solid rules in the home and the enforcement of these rules by consistent discipline. The remaining children in the home need the security of a well-structured family life based on a loving atmosphere and fair rules. You might turn back to chapter five and consider the list suggested there.

Ted Atkinson had prided himself in the philosophy of parenting with few rules. He had thought he was allowing his boys to learn to make decisions themselves, but he now realized that he had not given his sons enough guidance on how to make wise decisions and live according to Christian values.

Ted knew that he had a better opportunity to establish some rules now that Henry was out of the house. The key areas were curfews, dating rules, and use of drugs and alcohol.

Ted also established a new allowance system whereby the boys received their money only when they accomplished certain chores. Because of John's greater involvement in prodigal activity he was not allowed to work at an outside job until he had demonstrated a change in his behavior and had completed counseling concerning his drug use. Joe was allowed to mow lawns and seek other work outside the house.

2. *Effective Evangelism*

Now is the time to make sure that your other children have really been introduced to the gospel. Parents might want to review the strategy Kay Jamison used with her daughter, Joyce, (see page 00) so you can make use of any natural opening to talk about your faith.

As parents we need to remind ourselves that the gospel opens us up to God's love, giving us new life and the desire to obey God. The biblical writers give good reason for believing the gospel and obeying God's law. They never ask us to "just believe, don't ask questions." The following dynamics need to be applied if we want to pass on our faith to our children.

a. *We as parents are the Bible that our children read every day of their lives.* We can only pass on to our children the faith and character we ourselves possess. Jesus said that a disciple can not be greater than His teacher. If we have a weak and inconsistent faith, we should not expect more from our children. (Although by God's grace and other's influence this does occasionally happen.)

Donald Barnhouse commented that parents begin teaching their children about God 20 years before they are born. He meant that the parent's character, which was forming all those years, was the primary influence they would have on their children.[2] Thankfully, through the grace of God and the power of the gospel, we can be transformed into "new creatures" in Christ. This must be a manifested reality in our homes daily, and not merely put on as our "Sunday suit."

The first step we need to take is to draw near to God ourselves through Jesus Christ, repent of our sins, and strive to be spiritually consistent. Hypocrisy is the most frequent charge teenagers make against adults, and we must diligently guard against it in our own lives.

b. *We must be ready to have a "tough love" for our children.* This love will have the tenderness to give a loving touch and the toughness to give the necessary instruction and punishment needed to influence our children toward the proper values. This love will be one that perseveres even when they have been disobedient, ungodly, and unloving.

Such a love will only be reflected in our lives to the degree that we understand God's love for us. Our belief in God's love in Christ should so permeate our existence that our actions and reactions are instantly motivated by divine love toward our children. When we have developed such a "second nature," then Christian parenting stops merely being something we do and becomes something we are.

c. *Our children will learn, in a practical manner, most about their relationship with God within the personal interchange they have with other members of the family.* This is why I have stressed using the covenant as the basis of the home. As children see and experience love, chastisement, authority, rules, forgiveness, reconciliation, and intimacy in the home, they will be able to apply these to their relationship with God. We can portray a scaled down model of the drama of the biblical revelation in our homes if we contrast the main themes of the Bible with the most crucial elements of a home structured after the covenant.

Creation .... Birth or Adoption
Redemption .... Unconditional Love
                           and Forgiveness
Judgment .... Authority, Rules,
                           Chastisement, Blessing

Our homes can come to be concrete "sermons" which will be proclaimed to our children on a very deep and profound level.

d. *Christian parents tend to become moralistic and stress the "should/ought/must" of Christianity rather than the greatness of God our Creator, the revelation of God's love in Jesus Christ, and the tremendous value of God's kingdom.*

Our children need to hear us talking about what God has done, what God has said, and who God is rather than hearing constant "godly nagging" about being good. Being good is a "fruit" of having faith in Jesus and the presence of the Holy Spirit in our lives (Gal. 5:22–23). Sometimes we seem more concerned about our children's outward behavior than their faith and the attitude of their hearts. We must resist this temptation and work for a sincere heart faith and not mere outward conformity.

e. *Parents should not be concerned solely with their children's single "decision for Christ".* The real aim should be to foster a life of daily faith and repentance in their offspring. While this may begin with some outward confession of faith in Christ as Lord and Savior, it is a mistake to think that we can solve all the problems of our home by having our children make an emotional response to the gospel.

True faith is daily faith. True faith is growing faith. True faith is repentant faith. True faith manifests itself in a life of good deeds and ethical consistency. Being too "decision" oriented can put too much pressure on children to "make a choice," which only results in outward conformity rather than a true, heartfelt faith.

f. *We need to not only be concerned with teaching the content of the faith, but also about the process of living by faith.* Parents need to be empowering their children to make "faith-full" choices of discernment and obedience. The best defense against sexual sin, drunkenness, the use of drugs, and other sins is a self-discipline which demonstrates that the child has thought through the issues and made his or her own decision by God's grace to say no to these temptations.

The only answer to preventing the prodigal process or seeing a prodigal come home is to help our children "come to themselves."

3. Impressing on Our Children Their Personal Responsibility

Many parents accept the idea that one prodigal child produces another prodigal child. This thinking is then passed on to their children who use it as a cop-out for their own actions. This thinking must be rejected. The only person responsible to God for the rebellion is that particular child. The individual must be held accountable for his or her actions. Other siblings are not able to "cause" someone to become a prodigal. The issue of faith must be seen as between each child and Jesus Christ.

4. Seeking Help From Others

I often suggest that the parents and the prodigal (if he or she is still at home) look to others trained to reach young people with the gospel. Even Jesus said that "no prophet is accepted in his home town" (Luke 4:24, NIV). One way to do this is to send our children to a good Christian youth camp or caravan, which are often advertised in youth magazines like *Campus Life* or conducted by local churches. Such an experience will provide a good atmosphere where children can hear the gospel and at least for a time, be free of the pressures of living with a prodigal. Ted Atkinson sent his youngest son, Jim, on a youth caravan for one month that summer.

Parents also need to encourage a child to participate in the church's youth group. Jim Atkinson still wanted his father's approval more than his older brothers, so that fall Ted was able to get Jim to attend as many activities of the church youth group as possible. Ted, himself, became involved in the youth group by offering to be a chaperone at the ski weekend and then later participating in a Happening, a renewal weekend for young people, as a dad. Jim and his father became close friends as they participated in Happening activities for the next two years.

5. Drug and Sex Education

Two problems plaguing our young people and disrupting their lives to the greatest degree are sex and drugs. We cannot attempt to hide these issues in the closet any longer but must be willing to talk openly about these issues and help our children establish values based on a clear understanding of the facts and biblical revelation.

Researchers Robert Coles and Geoffrey Stokes also found that the strongest predictor of whether teenagers had sexual intercourse before marriage was whether or not they were influenced "a great deal" by religion. About 18 percent of kids said they had been influenced by religion, and 90 percent of those teens had never had intercourse. Once a teenager had engaged in sex, however, he nearly always continued. Only 6 percent of the nonvirgins surveyed had gone for more than a year without having intercourse again.[3]

Our child's response to the gospel on a deep personal level will be one of the major factors influencing him or her to remain sexually pure until marriage or help him or her refrain from being involved in a sexually active lifestyle outside marriage.

I recommend that parents (with a counselor's help if needed) tell their children all the problems sex outside of marriage and promiscuity can bring on them, and also tell them that they can remain free of sexual sin if they call upon God's grace. The U. S. Department of Health and Human Services has a useful pamphlet entitled "Many Teens Are Saying 'NO'," which would be good for parents to share with their children. At the end of the book I have listed other resources which may be of help in communicating proper ethical values about sex to teenagers. It would also be wise for parents to read Josh McDowell's book *Teens Speak Out: What I Wish My Parents Knew About My Sexuality*.

Parents need to become aware of drug education and rehabilitation programs in their local area. One drug program, Project 714, uses positive peer pressure as a weapon against drugs. This program, which was begun in Chattanooga, Tennessee, and has now spread to other states, begins with a Triple S Club—Students Staying Straight—in the local high school. Each club member must sign a contract, declaring abstinence from drugs and alcohol. The club holds regular meetings, during which the students discuss drug and alcohol abuse, and also sponsors school events which are drug-free. The local skating rink might open up its facilities to the group free of charge, for instance, and parents, instead of just dropping their kids off, take time to cook hot dogs with them.

Most of the Triple S Clubs have their own bulletin boards in the high school where they post both their events and a complete roster of their members, so students can monitor each other's activities to create a positive form of peer pressure.

In the spring of 1986, when the Chattanooga-area schools held their proms, Project 714 and several community groups featured a slogan contest. The winner received a "prom package" consisting of a complimentary dinner for two, a carriage ride in downtown Chattanooga, a fifty-dollar gift certificate toward the purchase of a dress, and a free tuxedo rental, all donated by local businesses. The winning slogan, "Impress Your Date—Drive Straight," along with the photograph of the winner, was featured on eight Chattanooga billboards.[4]

Project 714 was begun by Jimmy Lee, a former Teen Challenge staff member, who launched the program in 1981 because he believed that rehabilitation was reaching youth too late. Although the organization does not promote its religious perspectives on school grounds, the number 714 has its root in 2 Chronicles 7:14: "If My people who are called by My name will humble themselves, and pray and seek My face, and turn from their wicked ways, then I will hear from heaven, and will forgive their sin and heal their land." Jimmy Lee is, in fact, praying for a national turnaround.

Parents might look for Project 714 groups in their community or a program like this or they might wish to write to Jimmy Lee, Project 714, P. O. Box 8936, Chattanooga, Tennessee, 37411, (615-622-5724), and get the information to start a Triple S Club in their local high school.

One of the key principles of breaking the prodigal "chain reaction" is to become prevention-oriented, rather than waiting until our children have a problem.

6. Isolate these siblings from the influence of the prodigal

Bad company ruins good behavior, even when the influence is a brother or sister. If the prodigal continues his or her wild lifestyle, you may have to get the prodigal out of the home. Or if the prodigal has moved elsewhere, you might have to limit his or her opportunity to see younger brothers or sisters. Ted Atkinson told Henry that he was only to visit John and Jim when Ted or another trusted adult was at home.

7. Encourage new peer role models

We advised Ted Atkinson to introduce John to Gene Waite, one of the college students who helped with our church youth group. Gene visited the Atkinson's home several times, and then began to meet John on an individual basis.

It is best to make the introduction of a Christian youth leader or other positive role model as natural as possible. Having a bar-b-que at your home for some of the church youth and the youth minister can be a casual way to provide an opportunity for the two to meet. In other cases parents have opened up their homes for a Bible study and fellowship time for the youth department, bringing the influence and ministry of the youth director right into their living room. Talk to the youth leader and get his ideas. Any experienced youth worker has worked out ways of meeting kids in a casual and natural manner in order to build friendships and trust.

Even something as simple as a subscription to *Campus Life* magazine can help a teen see that some kids do make decisions based on their Christian beliefs. Although a prodigal like John Atkinson might not be interested in this magazine, Jim Atkinson was likely to read the magazine since he had not yet mimicked either of his brothers' behavior patterns.

Ted Atkinson was most successful with the younger boys. Whereas Henry came to talk to John and Jim a few times, he rarely spoke to his father, and when he did, they usually ended up having an argument. One time Henry threw a rock through a window of their house he was so angry.

Although John had at first sided with his brother, he was now touched by his dad's real concern for his sons—the late nights he walked the floors, the times he cried after a phone call from Henry ended in an argument, and the real effort he had made to spend time with John and Jim. His dad was now at home more often, making sure curfews were kept, and lovingly, but firmly taking away privileges and punishing behavior which was against the rules of the home. Ted had admitted that he had allowed work to overshadow his parenting responsibilities, and he had made it very clear to the boys through his actions that he was changing this situation.

Reinforcement is parents' most feared response to the prodigal process. While there are many concrete actions parents can take to stop the process from spreading to the other children, we must realize that we are not in full control of the situation. God must awaken within the child's heart the desire to seek His kingdom and His righteousness. Only divine intervention will ultimately save our children.

THIRD RESPONSE: RETREAT

Some siblings are torn between being loyal to their parents and being loyal to their prodigal brother or sister, so they simply retreat from deep relationships with either the prodigal or the parents. These siblings are afraid that a choice might lead to arguments and rejection, which they want to avoid, so they escape into their own private world.

As John Atkinson began to really respect his father, he felt torn between his father and his older brother, whom he still loved. John began to withdraw from his father by staying in his room much of the time and from his brother,

Henry, by refusing to answer the notes sent through their mutual friends.

When Henry did visit the family, John said very little, afraid that if he acted too friendly toward Henry his dad would think that he was siding with his brother. His reaction was harmful to himself, his dad, and Henry. John, who was now confused by the varying standards of his father and brother, needed his father's love. Instead he was cutting himself off from this important emotional and spiritual support. He even began to blame his dad for the new coldness in their relationship, although it was caused by his own actions.

John's retreat just added to his father's pain. Now there was a new wall of separation between Ted and his second son. Finally, John's neutrality was seen by Henry as rejection. John, by trying to avoid hurting anyone, was hurting both the prodigal and his dad.

Parents must not allow their child to isolate himself. We must also assure the child that he does not have to choose sides. Never force a child into any form of, "Whose side are you on?" If we do, he may retreat deeper, alienating himself further from us. Or he may feel so threatened that he decides to side with the prodigal.

THE PROPER RESPONSE: REDEMPTIVE RECONCILIATION

Parents should encourage the siblings to respond to the prodigal with redemptive, reconciling love. The other children in the family need to show concern for the prodigal and pray that he will turn from his sinful lifestyle. The siblings' proper response is to love the prodigal, hope for a reconciliation with the family, and refuse to give up their own Christian beliefs and ethical standards.

How can we really make our homes have an atmosphere of redemptive reconciliation? One helpful step is to consider the characteristics of strong families which are identified by Dr. Nick Stinnett, Dean of Pepperdine University. He studied a group of 3000 families that were determined to be "strong" in the opinion of family life experts and professional counselors. Three qualities the experts looked for were first and only marriages, a high degree of marital happiness, and an ability to meet each other's needs successfully.

The study revealed six crucial characteristics that appeared consistently in the 3000 families studied.[5] A family which is striving to keep the prodigal chain reaction from taking place could be aided in this effort by attempting to incorporate these six characteristics into their household.

The first characteristic that was found in these strong families is that they spend large amounts of time together. This is not something that happens by accident in these families, but is planned by the parents. I have already mentioned this, but it is further scientific confirmation of how important this aspect is to our dealing with the prodigal problem. Good families take lots of time.

The Bible makes clear that parents are responsible for family involvement in an instructive, productive, and edifying relationship centered around God and His Word. This should be done from the time they arise from sleep, all during the day, while sitting around the house in the evening at home, and until they go to sleep again at night. (See Deut. 6:7.) God intends for families to spend large amounts of time together.

Dr. Stinnett also found that successful families had good communication among their members. This good communication was based on two primary ingredients: first, lots of talking about everything from the sublime to the trivial, and secondly, a willingness to listen to each other.

This ability to communicate does not make families free of conflict, but enables them to be open about problems and to identify what is causing stress in the home. Open communication also allows families to focus on the problem rather than concentrating on mutual character assassination.

What will this mean to you practically as you fight to keep the prodigal chain reaction from sweeping through your house? One action you need to take is to turn off the television and get you and your children involved in other activities that allow more talking and interaction. Silence is not golden if you want to strengthen your home.

Good communication is one of the most crucial and yet the hardest skill to have in any family. To help you improve communication in your family, read Appendix 00, outlining how to set up a "family conference table" which has proven effective in helping people to express their thoughts and feelings to each other.

It is important to note that the families which researchers found to be "strong" seemed to be following biblical guidelines of communication even though they may not have been aware of the teaching of the Scriptures. These principles stress that we should be quick to listen, slow to speak, and slow to get angry (James 1:19–20; 3:1–18). The Scriptures teach us to use our speech to bring about reconciliation rather than conflict. God blesses those families which pattern themselves by His principles.

Thirdly, this study found that strong families had made a commitment to promoting each others' happiness and well-being and to unity. God commands strong family commitment (Exod. 20:12,14; Ephes. 6:1–4; Heb. 13:4). The family was the first institution that God created and is the God-ordained basis for society (Gen. 2:18–25). It continues to be the cornerstone of culture. Without strong families we cannot have strong churches nor strong governments. Only our commitment to Jesus Christ should come before our commitment to our families.

Parents can demonstrate their commitment to their children by eliminating their own activities for the sake of the family and by focusing on their children rather than the problem in the office or their favorite hobby. You need to stress family commitment even in the midst of the prodigal crisis. By talking about family commitment and unity you will help siblings to not totally reject the prodigal while remaining loyal to your standards and teachings. Having this characteristic in your homes is vital for the proper response of redemptive reconciliation to take place.

Interestingly, the fourth characteristic common among these 3000 families, one which Christians would expect to find, is that families need a feeling of spiritual wellness and religious orientation in order to be strong.

The faith found in strong families is not merely some type of abstract or theoretical faith, but a full-bodied, personal, practical faith that affects the everyday experience of family members. You cannot escape the necessity of leading your family by personal example into a dynamic and living faith in Jesus Christ.

Nothing will protect your children from the prodigal experience as well as a sincere, deep, genuine, personal commitment to Jesus as Lord and Savior that is consistently lived out. Pray that your home will be a center of "true spirituality" that will attract your children and their friends to Christ and His teachings. Such a reality in our homes will stop the prodigal chain reaction and produce redemptive, reconciling love.

It must be stressed here that strong families are not without crises. Many families studied have had to face the issue of a rebellious child or some other crisis. But strong families face such crises, not with despair, but in a positive manner. Even in the midst of pain and struggle, Dr. Stinnett found that successful families were able to see the silver lining in the midst of the trial. Sometimes this was simply becoming more aware of how much love and support existed in their family.

The crisis of having a prodigal child can be a positive experience as the parents and other children draw closer together and pray for the prodigal. This research points to the need of saturating your family with the attitude of "all things work together for good to those who love God."

Lastly, researchers found that it is important for family members to express sincere appreciation for each other. We can easily live with those we love the most and fail to give them a compliment for months. Sometimes even a simple "thank you" is rarely heard in families. By looking for the good in our children and taking time to let them know we do notice when they are doing well, we can keep the atmosphere of our home positive and encouraging even in the midst of struggle.

Homes that have prodigal children have a tendency to be predominated by a negative, critical, and even legalistic spirit. You must not allow this. Rather make your home a haven of love, support, and positive feedback for all the members of the family. You need to rebuke your children when they do wrong but you also need to praise them every time they do right.

Dr. Stinnett was surprised to find that positive reinforcement and support was such an important aspect in having a strong home. But from the viewpoint of the covenant structure of the home which we have used in this book, this evidence points out the essential importance of "the blessing" being stressed in your home as well as punishment when it is needed.

What exactly does it mean to "bless" our children? The

idea of blessing can be as simple as communicating appreciation on a regular basis and rewarding our children for obedience. But the blessing also needs to be seen in the deeper dimension of the biblical covenant. (See Deut. 28:1–14.) The book *The Blessing*, by Gary Smalley and John Trent, outlines five aspects of the biblical concept of blessing:[6]

- Meaningful Touch (Gen. 27:26)
- A Spoken Message
- Attaching "High Value" to the One Being Blessed (Gen. 27:27–29)
- Picturing a Special Future for the One Being Blessed (Gen. 28–29)
- An Active Commitment to Fulfill the Blessing

Communicate to your children through loving physical expressions (a hug, a kiss on the cheek, holding their hands) and tell them that they have been created by God, in His image, as a wonderfully unique person. Assure them that as they walk in faith in Jesus that God will work out His perfect plan in their lives. Promise them your prayers and support as a God-given helper in accomplishing God's plan in their life.

This type of positive affirmation of your children's importance to God is crucial for stopping the prodigal chain reaction which is usually based on the alluring "false blessings" offered by sin and the world. This positive, affirming, joyful, and promising atmosphere can be used greatly by God to stop a prodigal chain reaction.

Evaluate your home and see which of these six characteristics are lacking. Your parenting strategy should be aimed at working towards establishing these characteristics in your family. To further help you develop these traits in your family I have included an appendix on page

226, by Christian counselor Wayne Mack, which should be of help.

In his report, Dr. Stinnett pointed out that some of these strong families had once been extremely weak, even on the verge of completely falling apart. Perhaps that is how you view your family today. How did these weak families become strong? They decided to change and make the family a main concern of their time, energy, and prayers. This choice turned them around. The same may happen in your home, even in the midst of the prodigal process, even as you face the danger of having a prodigal chain reaction, if you will dedicate your family to God and make its success a priority. While such a decision does not guarantee success in solving the prodigal problem, it is an important step to take as a family.

How did Ted's three sons respond to his efforts to stop the prodigal chain reaction? Henry went to college, but dropped out after his freshman year. In the next years, he worked at some fairly good jobs but lost them because of insubordination or sloppy work. Yet his handsome appearance and winning personality always enabled him to find new positions. So far Henry has never changed his lifestyle.

Both John and Jim experimented with marijuana and sexual relationships during their high school years. Yet, their dad's persistent love, discipline, and concern kept them from adopting a lifestyle of promiscuity and drug abuse. Before they graduated from high school, they both professed to having accepted Christ as Savior and vowed to follow a Christian lifestyle. Ted Atkinson and his boys still maintain a relationship with Henry, though they are not as close to him as they would like to be. They are still waiting for their prodigal to return home.

12

How Can Prodigals Keep From Having Prodigals?

Unfortunately, statistics show that children often repeat a parent's life pattern. Women who become pregnant out of wedlock find, more often than not, that their daughters repeat their mistake. The children of alcoholics have a greater likelihood of becoming alcoholics. Children whose parents are divorced are more likely to divorce. Young people who suffered sexual and physical abuse from their parents too often end up committing the same abhorrent crimes against their children. These sad patterns of behavior demonstrate that the sins of the parents can influence children to repeat the same mistakes.

Sam Giglotti was very worried about this when he came to see one of our counselors. Sam's dad was an alcoholic. Even though his parents argued constantly, Sam had never thought his parents would get a divorce because his mother was a committed Christian. Yet they did. Sam was moved from his home, separated from his friends, and placed in a totally new environment.

His mother felt as if she had failed, and this feeling was reinforced by the many church members who shunned her because of the divorce. Sam vowed that he would never get a divorce or drink alcohol. During his high-school years he had successfully resisted the pressure to drink, protesting, "Drinking is not for me. I've seen what it can do to people and I want no part of it."

In college his friends also urged him to drink. These friends were Christians, who ridiculed him for not using his "liberty." They would say to him, "Sam, you are just hung up on tradition. There is no verse that says you can't have a drink if you want to. Your dad's drinking wouldn't have been a problem if he'd drunk in moderation. You need to loosen up and be free in Christ."

Eventually, Sam listened to their misguided counsel and decided to try a beer. When no harm seemed to come of it, he was amazed. He started to have wine with his meals occasionally.

His girlfriend, Sally, was also a "liberated Christian." Her parents had been divorced, so she shared Sam's determination to have a lasting marriage. Both of them made this vow before their wedding.

For a while they remained true to their vows. Then they began to fight over relatively small matters. Sally would get hysterical, claiming Sam was "just like my dad who left me when I was six." As their unhappiness increased, both Sam and Sally began to drink excessively. Sally lost several jobs, and even when she was without work, she let the housework go. Instead, she spent her time reading different books on philosophy.

The Giglottis sought marriage counseling, but nothing seemed to help them resolve their problems. One counselor told them, "The two of you are headed in different directions. You think differently, believe differently, have different priorities, and define marriage differently. And neither of you is willing to change! It will take a miracle to save this union."

That miracle did not occur. One day Sally told Sam that she no longer believed in marriage. "I've been seeing a couple of guys. I don't want to be married any longer. I have filed for divorce."

THE DESTRUCTIVE CHAIN

Many people fear, as Sam did, that they will repeat their parents' mistakes, and, as I mentioned at the beginning of this chapter, their fears are valid since statistics do indicate this cycle. This pattern can also be found in the Bible.

Perhaps the most vivid illustration is found in the lives of David and his son Solomon. David, a godly man, allowed the sin of lust to tempt him to become an adulterer and a murderer. Solomon, the son of David and Bathsheba (the woman David with and for whom David committed these sins), obviously had problems controlling his passion. He created a royal harem of one thousand wives and concubines, many of whom were pagans. These wives finally drew his loyalty away from the God of Israel so that he allowed idol worship. Even though this father and son had very different personalities, both of them were tempted by sexual sins.

David truly repented of his sins. Yet his ungodly example influenced two of his sons, Solomon and Absolom. Many parents who were prodigals themselves harbor the fear that their children will repeat their mistakes.

FAITH NOT FEAR

The first advice I gave to Sam was that old faithful exhortation: do not panic. "You have to calm down and recognize that you can only break this chain by faith, not fear. Fear will make you overreact, block any rational thought, and tempt you to try to control the situation through your own actions rather than trust God to solve the problem."

Together Sam and I reflected on his life. His first mistake Sam felt, was in compromising his conscience by hanging around with a "liberated crowd" in college. Once he began to drink, his use of alcohol had gone way beyond moderation and contributed to the destruction of his marriage. Because he had wandered from his Christian upbringing, Sam had never thought to look to God to save his marriage; instead, he had relied on his own actions.

Sam began to see that he should never have married Sally since she had always rebelled against authority in college and in her Christian life. His strong physical attraction to her had overridden the warnings of friends, family, and counselors who had advised them against marriage. This, he knew now, was a result of his pride that had him think, *I know more than all of them, and this marriage will not fail.* The divorce humbled Sam and made him fearful of continuing to make poor decisions.

During counseling, Sam decided to recommit his life to Christ and give Him control of the future. Eventually Sam married a Christian woman, Naomi. Their marriage reflected the reality of a Christ-centered home, which Sam had always desired. Both he and Naomi were overjoyed when they had a son, Denny, four years later.

However, Sam became deeply concerned that his little boy might repeat his own errors, becoming the third generation to be caught in this destructive pattern. Again, Sam came to the church for counseling. "I'm so happy to be a father," he told his counselor, "but when I look at Denny, I'm filled with fear. I know that the troubles in life are my own responsibility, but nevertheless, I followed my dad's pattern. How can I keep Denny from making the same mistake?"

USING YOUR MISTAKES IN A POSITIVE WAY

God has promised that "All things work together for good to those who love God" (Rom. 8:28). If children of prodigals identify the factors that led them to choose the wrong path, they can develop individual parenting strategies to help their children avoid these errors. Their mistakes will "work together for good" for their children.

"Your divorce caused you to see many areas of failure in your life," our counselor told Sam. "This kind of knowledge and the deep insight you gained from admitting your sins can be one of the most valuable treasures you can pass on to your son. The truths we learn in the pig pen are much more vivid to us than those we read about in psychology books. You need to ask God to transform your mistakes into wisdom so you can pass that on to your son as he grows up."

In the next weeks of counseling, Sam isolated the key temptations that had led him to sin:

- A surrender to peer pressure, despite his own conscience.
- Pride
- Uncontrolled sexual passion
- A failure to follow Christ as Lord.

With this knowledge, Sam was able to develop a parenting strategy to reinforce the truths that would equip him to face and overcome these temptations. Sam and the counselor identified three influences that had equipped Sam to change his lifestyle:

1. The "megaphone" of God shouting at him in the midst of his adversity.

2. The biblical teaching of pastors who had helped him understand his sins and how to be freed from them.

3. The determination to take time for reflective moments of prayer and sober thinking. This allowed him to fuse the teaching of the Bible and the insights he had

gained from God's working in his life through the power of the Holy Spirit into the strong alloy of Christian character.

Sam's parenting strategy was to change these influences into positive steps that he and his wife could follow as they reared their son.

1. Use Controlled Adversity to Teach the Child

Since Sam did not want Denny to have to make the mistakes he had, he used "controlled adversity" to teach his son lessons as he grew up. These lessons would be much more painful if they were left to be learned from the bigger mistakes he would make as an adult.

Our counselor suggested that Sam and his wife allow Denny to pay the price of irresponsible behavior as he grew up. The Giglottis applied this concept one day when after he watched his mother take an aspirin for a headache, Denny asked if he could take one.

"I want some of the candy!" Denny insisted.

"It's not candy," Naomi replied. "It doesn't taste good. It's medicine to take when you have a headache as I do now."

Still, Denny demanded, "I want that candy!"

Sam, who was listening to this conversation, looked over at Naomi to indicate that he wanted to become a part of the argument. Then he wisely said, "Okay, since you will not listen, I will let you have this medicine so you will learn to believe your mother and me."

Naomi gave Denny an aspirin. His eyes lit up. Candy! Quickly he grabbed the tablet and bit into it, expecting the sweet taste of sugar. Instead he tasted the bitterness of the chemicals.

He spit out the candy, and quickly asked to have a glass of water. "It doesn't taste good!" he wailed.

After Denny drank some water, his dad sat him on his lap. "Mom and I love you dearly. When we tell you something is bad for you, please listen. We only say these things to keep you from being hurt." By reinforcing this lesson with an explanation, Sam and Naomi turned a potentially frustrating experience into a powerful and useful lesson.

2. Use Biblical Teaching to Help the Child Understand Sin and Forgiveness

Children can also learn biblical principles through the events of their everyday lives if their parents pattern these principles in their own lives.

Our counselor spoke to Sam about the benefits of confession and forgiveness. "One of the main reasons you have been able to get your life together is that you faced the sins you committed, accepted your responsibility for them, confessed them, and received forgiveness. This cycle is vital for anyone's spiritual and emotional health. It allows each of us to be free of the past and to press on toward the hope of the future. You need to teach Denny to do this by your example."

All too often we believe that we must present the image of being perfect parents, beyond reproach. However, as Christians, we know that it is a lie to claim to be without sin (see 1 John 1:8–10). Therefore, when we sin against our children, we should be willing to ask them for forgiveness.

By doing this, we teach our children that God's principles apply to everyone. If we ask them for forgiveness, our children will find it easier to ask us to forgive them. Communication with someone who admits his mistakes is easier than with someone we consider to be far better than we are. By living out the Gospel before our children, we can help them avoid self-righteousness and prevent an improper idolization of us as parents.

Sam was able to put this principle in practice one day when he ate a bag of Denny's candy, which was lying on the kitchen table. As Naomi was taking the little boy to his room for a nap, he had asked his dad, "Don't eat that candy. I'm saving it for my treat." Sam had promised his son, but later had become so involved in his paperwork that he had absent-mindedly forgotten his son's request and eaten the candy.

Immediately after Denny woke up from his nap, he walked into the kitchen, still rubbing his sleepy eyes. "Candy?" he asked, looking toward the kitchen table. When he reached up on the table for his candy, he found the empty bag. He crushed the paper bag in his hands and began to scream.

Sam faced a decision all parents face at one time or another. He could shout down his son, threatening to punish him if he would not be quiet. (*After all,* he could rationalize, *I bought the candy so I ought to be able to have some if I want it.*) Or he could admit his mistake. Sam knew that in his son's eyes, Daddy had stolen the candy.

Sam took Denny into his arms and comforted him until he quieted down. Then he said, "I am sorry, please forgive me. Daddy was wrong. I should not have eaten your candy." He added, "Lord Jesus, forgive me for taking Denny's candy."

Denny blinked at his dad, sniffling. "Will . . . you . . . get me some more?"

Sam smiled, "Yes, I will. I'll even buy you two bags to make it up to you! Will you forgive me?" he asked Denny again.

Denny smiled back at his dad. "I forgive you, Daddy. Will Jesus forgive you?"

Sam was amazed at his son's discernment. "Yes, Jesus will forgive me when I tell him I am sorry for doing wrong and will not do it again. He has promised He will."

Denny thought about his father's words for a moment, and then said, "Let's go get the candy!"

3. Encourage the child to take time for reflective moments of prayer and thinking

Sam and Naomi were going to visit their best friends, Kim and Harry Bright. The Brights had a son, Martin, who loved to play with Denny. However, the boys often got too rowdy and the parents often had to discipline the children rather than enjoy adult conversation at the Brights'.

Sam drove up to the Brights' house, parked the car, and turned to Denny. Already the young boy's eyes were aglow with the anticipation of playing with his friend. Sam said, "Denny, do you remember the last time you came to visit Martin? You two boys had to spend so much time standing in the corner because you would not calm down and play right."

Denny's smile vanished. "Yea, Daddy, I remember. But I will be good. I promise."

"Denny, I know you will try to be good, but you need to ask Jesus to help you to play right so that you won't have to be punished like you were before. It will only take a minute and we can do it right now."

Sam bowed his head. Denny imitated his dad and said "Jesus help me be good and not have to stand in the corner. Thank you for this beautiful day. Amen." Sam gave his son a hug and took him into the house to play with Martin. Jesus answered that prayer. The boys had never been as good as they were that day.

By praying often in this manner with their son, Sam

and Naomi hope to encourage Denny to take time to pray and to recognize that he needs to think about the Lord's will before he acts.

THE FUTURE IS NOT GOVERNED BY THE PAST

Parents must realize that their children's future is not governed by the parents' past. What we *were* is not as important as what we *are*. If parents are giving their children the most positive Christian example they can, they are doing all that can be done.

Our counselor admitted to Sam, "No one can argue against statistics. We can influence our children in the wrong way. But God's grace in Jesus is greater than our sins. You are not like your father. Your home is governed by God's love and His law much more than your parents' home was, even after the divorce. You must entrust the future to God and walk faithfully and consistently with Him every day. This is all you can do, and all that God expects of you."

Parents do not have to fear that the past has some sort of magical power to determine their children's future. Rather, they can walk in faith, knowing that the power of the gospel is stronger than any other force in the world. Even if their children do repeat their sins and suffer as they suffered, this does not mean that their lives will be unsuccessful. If God used hard times to soften the parents and make them more like Christ, He can do the same for their children. Parents cannot keep their children from experiencing pain in our fallen world, but they can pray that the pain will be redemptive and awaken their children to their need for Jesus.

Sam and a counselor from the Coral Ridge Ministries continued to meet a few times a year to reinforce the principles I have mentioned in this chapter. Several years later, in their final counseling session, Sam said, "I really appreciate your helping me cope with my fear. I do not always succeed as a parent, but I have confidence that God is active in my life and in Denny's.

"That song we sang last night at prayer service sums up my feelings. The chorus said, 'I do not know the future, but I know the One who holds the future in His hands.' That means a lot more to me now that I am raising a child. Praise God I can trust Him for the future and continue to grow in His grace!"

13

A Reason for Hope

I would like to leave you with one last story of hope. It happened as this book was being written. Pete Smith, an active member of Coral Ridge Church, shared with me an experience that occurred in a home Bible study he teaches Friday nights.

Jill was a girl who had gone through some very hard times. She had gone down the road of drug abuse and wild living. In high school she had started drinking heavily and would get drunk frequently on weekends. During high school she started partying heavily and became sexually active. Her sister and father, who were Christians, prayed for her, counseled her, and attempted to get her to see the destructive nature of her lifestyle. Jill resisted all of this advice. She told her sister, "Get off my back. Just because you want to be a virgin doesn't mean I have to miss out on having fun."

When Jill got out of high school, she got a job in a restaurant. She began hanging around a rough crowd and soon her partying included the use of marijuana and other drugs.

After a while, Jill tired of short-term sexual affairs, and she longed for someone who could take away her feelings of loneliness. Then she met Tom at the restaurant and began dating him. Tom drank a little but did not use drugs. Jill straightened out her life and cut back on her use of alcohol and drugs, because she did not want to lose Tom. After they were married, Jill returned to the destructive use of alcohol and drugs. Her lifestyle frustrated Tom, but he felt powerless to change their unhappy existence. Soon they separated.

Through the advice and encouragement of family and friends, Jill began to recognize that the alcohol and drug abuse were hurting her life. She committed herself to a drug rehabilitation program and kicked her addiction. Yet, even though she felt better about herself, she was still empty inside; she felt deeply that there had to be more to life than she had experienced.

The week she was released from the drug program, her sister, Paula, invited Jill to attend Pete's home Bible study. She agreed.

Paula and Jill came early to the study, and Jill had time to meet and speak with Pete before class began. Making small talk, she asked, "What do you for a living?"

He answered "I'm a Christian counselor. It is a great challenge. The needs of people are so great, but I do what I can to help people find answers to their problems by looking to God's grace in Jesus Christ."

"Oh! You're in counseling," Jill replied. "Maybe we could talk later. I've just graduated from a drug program and have been clean for the last twelve weeks. I believe in God, but I really feel I need to know Him a lot better. My husband and I are separated, and I have some other problems I'd like to discuss."

"I'll be glad to meet with you right after the meeting. Make sure you stay around until I'm free so we can really talk." Pete put his arm around Jill's shoulder and gave her a hug.

Pete's topic that night was "Three Keys to Spiritual Growth," which pointed out the need to look for God in the midst of all our experiences and adversities, to cultivate an awareness of God's presence by listening to His Word, to take time to meditate on who God is and what He has done. Pete ended the lesson by saying, "When we want to know who God is, let us remember to look to Jesus Christ. He was God Incarnate; in Him we have seen God become flesh. Let us take time to meditate on Jesus, for in Him we can see most clearly what God has done for us, who He is, and what He has said! My friends, turn your eyes to Jesus and trust in Him."

After the study Pete and Jill were able to find a quiet corner where they could talk. Jill told him, "I really enjoyed your talk. But I don't know if I understand all of it. I mean, I do believe in God, and I am trying to live a good life, at least right now. But what is this my sister and father mean about being born again? Is there more to that than just being good?"

Pete smiled and replied, "Jill, I'm glad that you believe in God and that you are trying to get your life straightened out. But to be born again means a lot more than just believing in some God out there and trying to do the best we can. We are born again when the Holy Spirit opens our eyes to see Jesus as our personal Prophet, Priest, and King. This new birth causes us to be committed to Jesus as our Lord and Savior. We walk a new life of faith, not being self-righteous, but reflecting God's righteousness in our lives. Would you like me to explain to you what it means to believe in Jesus as your Lord and Savior?"

"Yes, I really would," Jill replied without hesitation. "I feel like God brought me here tonight just to get the answers I'm looking for!"

"Good! I believe that, too." Pete continued with the gospel. "First, to accept Jesus as Prophet you need to believe that He was God in the flesh and that He demonstrated who God was through His life and teaching. You must personally commit yourself to be willing to accept what Jesus says to be true. Do you think you understand that now?"

Jill nodded that she did.

"Fine. Now, to accept Jesus as Priest means that you must totally reject the idea that you can save yourself by your good works and instead must rely only on the death of Jesus Christ on the cross as the payment for your sins. The wages of our sins was death and punishment in hell, but Jesus took that pain upon Himself on the cross. He took our place and paid for the sins of His people. God confirmed this by physically raising Him from the dead. Does that make sense to you?"

Jill said thoughtfully, "I know I've messed up. I need forgiveness badly. And I need my husband to forgive me for all I have put him through. I know that except for God's working in my life I would still be on drugs. Yes, I need Jesus to save and forgive me. That is for sure!"

Pete nodded in agreement. "It is so important that you see that clearly." He continued, "Finally, you must also accept Jesus as the King of your life. You must believe that God has raised Him up and given Him all authority and power. You must personally submit to Jesus and be willing to attempt the best you can to follow Him as the ruler of your life. This means that from now on, Jesus is boss. Does that make sense?"

"Yes, Pete, it does. I haven't done very well being my own boss. I need Jesus to be my leader and show me how to live each day."

"Jill, if you sincerely believe in Jesus as your Prophet, Priest, and King, then you need to call out to Him in prayer and ask Him to save you. Remember He is alive, and can hear your prayers. He has promised that 'Whosoever calls upon the name of the Lord shall be saved.' Let's do that right now."

Pete and Jill bowed their heads in prayer, calling upon

Jesus for His forgiveness and salvation. Afterward, as Jill got up and walked into the kitchen she announced, "I've just accepted Jesus!" Paula came over and hugged her sister. She and her father had been praying for years to see Jill come to this point.

Jill now meets with Pete weekly and learns more about the Lord and the life of faith. She also attends home Bible studies and Sunday school and has even begun to witness at the retail store where she works as a cashier. When fellow employees invite her to weekend parties she tells them, "I can't come. I have gone to more parties than I can count, and I never really found happiness at any of them. But I have found Jesus Christ, and my life has a peace that drugs could never give. Maybe we can talk about it sometime." A few of them have talked to Jill privately and asked her about her changed life. One girl, Kimmy, asked Jill to pray for her to be free of cocaine addiction. Already God is using Jill to touch others with His grace.

If you had met Jill a year ago, you might have felt she was beyond redemption. Yet God reached her in the midst of the darkness of drugs and brought her into the light to see Jesus.

My friend, the same can be true of your prodigal child, wherever they may be, whatever they have done, and no matter how far away from God they appear to be. The good news of the gospel can still reach them, and the Holy Spirit can still open their eyes. Do not despair, but hope and pray for the day when your prodigal will come home and you can say, "It was right that we should make merry and be glad, for your brother was dead and is alive again, and was lost and is found" (Luke 15:32).

APPENDIX 1

Five Steps to Evangelizing Your Child

The following conversation between a youngster named Sue and myself outlines five steps to evangelize your child

1. Present the concept of *Grace* (Eph. 2:8,9; Rom. 6:23)

Heaven is a Free Gift: It is not earned or deserved.

I often begin by asking, "What would you say to God if He asked why He should let you into heaven?"

Sue replied, "I tried to do the best I could. I lived a good life."

"Well, then, I have some really good news for you. In fact, I would go so far as to say that in the next sixty seconds you are going to hear the greatest news you have ever heard in your whole life! That's quite a statement, isn't it?"

The only answer to that question is yes. And Sue replied, "It certainly is."

"For a large part of my life I felt exactly as you feel. *If I'm going to get to heaven, I'm going to have to earn it. Become good enough. Work hard.* Then I discovered something that absolutely amazed me. Heaven is a free gift. Unearned and unmerited. Free! There's a verse in the Bible that tells us this. Ephesians 2:8–9. Would you read it, Sue?"

I handed Sue a Bible open to Ephesians 2, and she read the verses. "For by grace you have been saved through faith, and that not of yourselves; it is a gift of God, not of works, lest anyone should boast."

"You're probably thinking, *How can that be?*"

217

2. Help the Person Understand Man's Situation (Rom. 3:23)

Man Is A Sinner: He cannot save himself.

"In Romans 3:23 the Bible tells us that we have all sinned. Not one of us is good enough to get to heaven because God's standard is perfect. (Jesus said, "Be you therefore perfect, even as your Father which is in heaven is perfect.") None of us can earn our way into heaven.

"This is even more obvious when we understand what God is like."

3. Help the Person to Understand God's Nature (Rom. 2:1–5)

God is Merciful and Just.

"The Bible gives us two pictures of God, which at first seem contradictory. He is merciful and loving, gracious and kind. Yet He is also just, holy, and righteous. The Bible says that God is angry with the wicked every day, and that He commands all men everywhere to repent.

"God devised a solution to this dilemma. He sent His Son into the world to solve this problem for man."

4. Help the Person to Understand Christ's Mission (John 1:1–14; Isaiah 53:6)

Christ is the infinite God-Man.

"According to the Bible, Jesus Christ is God, the second person of the Trinity, the Creator of the universe. The Bible says, 'In the beginning was the Word and the Word was with God, and the Word was God. . . . And the Word became flesh and dwelt among us.'"

He paid for our sins.

"The entire Bible focuses on one great transaction." As I said this I held out my Bible to Susan. "Imagine that this book in my right hand contained a minute-by-minute account of my life—all my sins, my thoughts, my motives.

"The Bible tells us that someday the books will be opened and everybody will know all about us, everything we've ever done in secret. That's going to be a red-faced day for many. If any man is judged according to what's recorded in this book, he will be condemned.

"Our sin, which is written in this book, is our problem," I said. Now I placed the book on the palm of one hand. "Our sin is on us like a great burden. It keeps us out of heaven."

I held out my free hand. "Suppose my other hand represents Jesus Christ. The Bible says God placed all our sins on Jesus." Now I transferred the book to my free hand. "All our guilt, all our sin.

"God poured out all His wrath for our sin on His own Son. Imagine that! The Bible says, 'It pleased the Lord to bruise him.' As a parent I could hardly believe that. What a sacrifice!

"Jesus, through His suffering on the cross, paid for our sin. Now He's gone to prepare a place for us in heaven. He offers this place to each of us as a gift. To accept this gift we must have faith in Jesus as our Lord and Savior."

5. Help the Person to Understand Faith (John 6:47; 1 John 5:13)

Faith is not a mere intellectual assent.

"Lots of people believe that Jesus lived and died and rose again. They suppose that this is faith. But it's just an intellectual assent to certain historical facts. Even the devil believes in Christ this way.

"Other people trust Christ for the temporal things of life—health, guidance, strength—and they think they have faith. But real faith means to trust Christ for our salvation, life in the hereafter as well as life today. Christ didn't come to earth just to help us get through an operation or have a safe trip to New York City. He came to earth so we might have eternal life."

Faith is trusting in Jesus Christ alone for salvation.

"People tend to trust one of two options: either themselves or Christ. I used to trust in my own efforts to try to live a good enough life, just as you probably are. Then I realized that if I could get myself to heaven in this way, I would save myself; and if I could save myself, I would be my savior; and if I were my savior, then I would be in competition with Jesus Christ who claimed to be the Savior of the World.

"I needed to cease trusting in myself and start trusting in Jesus Christ. And so, years ago, I did just that, and I received the gift of eternal life. I didn't deserve it then, and I don't deserve it now, but by His grace I have it!"

I got up and pointed to an empty chair. "Let me illustrate this with this chair. Do you believe this chair exists?"

"Yes," Sue said.

"Do you believe it will hold you?" I asked.

"Yes."

"It is not holding you now. How could you prove that it exists and can hold you?"

Sue responded, "By sitting in it."

I nodded in agreement. "Let the chair represent Jesus Christ. For a long time I believed He existed and could help me, but I did not have eternal life, because I was trusting my own good works to get me into heaven.

"Remember what you told me you'd say to God if He asked, 'Why should I let you into heaven?' You said, 'I tried to do the best I could.'

"Who is the person referred to in your answer?"

Sue thought for a moment. "Me?"

"Who were you trusting to get you into heaven?"

"Why me!" she quickly responded.

"To receive eternal life, Sue, you must transfer that trust from yourself to Christ."

Faith is accepting Jesus Christ as the ruler of our lives.

"I'm sure you're wondering then, *If eternal life is a gift, why do I have to live a godly life?* Because of our gratitude to Christ for this gift. The Bible says, 'the love of Christ constrains us.'

"A former president of Princeton put it this way: 'As a young man I accepted Christ and the gift of eternal life. All the rest of my life was simply a P. S. to that day, saying, 'Thank you, Lord, for what you gave to me then.'

"Does that make sense to you, Sue?"

"Oh, yes," she cried, "that's wonderful!"

"You've just heard the greatest story ever told, about the greatest offer ever made, by the greatest Person who ever lived.

"Now the question is this: Do you want to receive this gift of eternal life that Christ gives you?"

Sue answered, "Oh, yes, I do."

Together Sue and I prayed that she would receive Christ as her Lord and Savior.

Parents should memorize the five steps and general outline and corresponding Scriptural references, which will organize their thoughts and enable them to clearly share the gospel with their children. This outline should not be mechanically shared but incorporated into the testimony of the faith of the parents. This is an abbreviated outline based on the outline used by tens of thousands of people trained in my Evangelism Explosion method. It has proven to be a useful tool in explaining God's love to others and could be a vital help in sharing our faith with our children. I would recommend for a complete understanding of how to share your faith that you obtain a copy of my book, *Evangelism Explosion*. You might also share this book with your pastor, and encourage him to begin this lay witnessing program in your church.

To get more information on Evangelism Explosion, please write to:

Evangelism Explosion International, III
5554 N. Federal Hwy.
Ft. Lauderdale, Fl. 33308

APPENDIX II

The Family Conference Table

PURPOSE

The *Family Conference Table* is to help families develop the ability and habit of communicating in a Christian manner for mutual edification and to solve interpersonal and family problems on a biblical basis.

GOALS

1. Reestablish and strengthen family communication
2. Bring family closer together
3. Find biblical solutions to conflicts and problems
4. Provide biblical structure for effective communication
5. Provide a place for regular communication
6. Provide an alternative to arguments
7. Provide a teaching center for learning to speak the truth in love.

PLACE

The parents should choose a table that is not used for other purposes and which can be designated the "Family Conference Table." They may want to set up a card table just for this purpose.

Appendix II

PREPARATION

Parents should discuss how they will conduct their Family Conference Table. I recommend you read *The Use of the Scriptures in Counseling* by Jay Adams and published by Presbyterian and Reformed Publishing Company. In Chapter 10, Dr. Adams explains the conference table. *Repentance and 20th Century Man,* by C. John Miller, published by Christian Literature Crusade, will also be helpful. These books are brief, easy to understand, and provide concrete direction in finding biblical answers to your everyday problems.

BIBLICAL PRINCIPLES TO FOLLOW

All communication during the meeting is to conform to the following biblical standards:

* Scripture as your authority and basis for conduct (2 Tim. 3:16–17)
* Be truthful (Eph. 4:15,25)
* Be loving (Eph. 4:15)
* Do not react in anger (i.e., blow-up or clam up) Eph. 4:26, 29, 31)
* Be kind (Eph. 4:32; 1 Pet. 3:9)
* Do not use unwholesome words, but only those that will build up others (Eph. 4:29)
* Do not argue (2 Tim. 2:23,24; Titus 3:9)
* Focus only on dealing with yourself, not on changing the other family members (Exod. 18:20; Matt. 7:1–5)
* Be forgiving (Eph. 4:32; Mark 11:25–26)

HOW TO DO IT

The head of the household should establish a regular time and frequency for the meetings (at least once a week). Meetings should be kept short. They should never go over an hour unless all are agreed that the time is being well spent. The family meeting should begin and end in prayer. It would be good to start each meeting with the reading of a Scripture passage dealing with biblical communication, such as Ephesians 4:17–32.

The first meeting should be committed to the confession of one's own sins. Each person needs to make a list of sins he has committed against each member of the family. The head of the family should begin by confessing his sins and asking forgiveness of those wronged. Every member of the family should follow this pattern. Stress the fact that though the issue may not be resolved, every member of the family needs to forgive those who have sinned against him. He should not hold feelings of bitterness or hurt.

For the second meeting each person should come with suggestions about how he can improve himself. Each person should again confess any new sins and ask forgiveness of those offended. Every member of the family should help the others with ideas for solving their problems in a godly manner.

At the first few conferences, each family member will focus on confessing *only* his own sinful behavior against others present (Matt. 7:1–5), asking for forgiveness (Matt. 5:23–24), and doing whatever may be necessary for reconciliation. (This will include restitution, asking others present if they remember any sins that the one confessing has not mentioned, asked forgiveness for, or asked for help in changing, etc.) However, remember that confessing one's own sins at the conference table needs to be voluntary. No one should force another to confess his or her sins. Convicting one of sin and prompting him to repent of it are the Holy Spirit's responsibility. (See John 14:26; 16:8–9.) The willingness to deal with one's own sins is each person's responsibility (Ezek. 18:20).

If anyone begins to argue, clam up, or become sarcastic or verbally abusive, all other family members should stand up as a signal that he or she is no longer communicating in a biblical manner. The offender should stop whatever he or she (or they) was doing wrong, indicate a willingness to talk, and invite the others to be seated. If the offender refuses to comply, then stop the conference. You may wait until the next scheduled meeting to continue, or if the offender repents beforehand, reconvene at your earliest convenience.

This same procedure may be followed if, during the conference, someone becomes angry or emotional. The person could stand, indicating a need to stop talking until emotions can be brought under control. The family member may have to excuse himself or herself from the conference for the time needed to gain control (Eph. 4:26).

At the conclusion of each meeting, each person should pray, asking for God's forgiveness and strength to turn from personal sins (1 John 1:8–9; Prov. 28:13).

Key Points to keep in mind:

1. Attack problems not people (Eph. 4:29–31).
2. Keep control of your temper (Prov. 15:28, 14:17, 29).
3. Seek to solve problems daily (Luke 9:23).
4. Do not use abusive language.
5. Pray at the beginning and end of the Family Conference.
6. Look for specific biblical answers to the problems raised. (Keep an open Bible on the table.*)
7. Discuss your own failures.
8. Humbly seek the advice of other family members.
9. Look for specific ways of solving problems.
10. Be quick to stand up at the table if tempers flare or communication is broken off.
11. Stress the command "do not let the sun go down on your wrath" (Eph. 4:26).

(*It would be helpful to use a *Nave's Topical Bible*. I also recommend you use *The Christian Counselor's New Testament,* by Jay Adams, and a *Strong's Concordance,* both of which will facilitate locating specific passages on different problems and issues.)

APPENDIX III

How To Raise A Child For God

Study the following principles and circle the ones where you are failing.[1]

1. Examine your expectations for your child. Are they realistic? Evaluate them in the light of the Bible (1 Cor. 13:11; Matt. 18:10; Gen. 33:12–14).
2. Love him unconditionally (Deut. 7:7; 1 John 4:10,19).
3. Look for opportunities in which you can commend him. Express appreciation for him frequently (Phil. 1:3; 1 Thess. 1:2; 2 Thess. 1:3).
4. Seldom criticize without first expressing appreciation for good points (1 Cor. 1:3–13).
5. Give him freedom to make decisions where serious issues are not at stake. Your goal should be to bring your child to maturity in Christ and not to dependence on you (Eph. 4:13–15; 6:4; Prov. 22:6; Col. 1:27–28).
6. Do not compare him with others (Gal. 6:4; 2 Cor. 10:12–13; 1 Cor. 12:4–11).
7. Never mock him or make fun of him. Do not demean or belittle your child. Beware of calling him dumb or clumsy or stupid (Matt. 7:12; Eph. 4:29–30; Col. 4:6; Prov. 12:18; 16:24).
8. Do not scold him in front of others (Matt. 16:22–23; 18:15; 1 Cor. 16:14).
9. Never make threats or promises that you do not intend to keep (Matt. 5:37; James 5:12; Col. 3:9).

10. Don't be afraid to say "no," and when you say it, mean it (Prov. 22:15; 29:15; 1 Sam. 3:13; Gen. 18:19).
11. When your child has problems or is a problem, do not overreact or lose control of yourself. Do not yell or shout or scream at him (Eph. 4:26–27; 1 Cor. 16:14; 2 Tim. 2:24–25; 1 Tim. 5:1–2)).
12. Communicate optimism and expectancy. Do not communicate by word or action that you have given up on your child and are resigned to his being a failure (Philem. 21; 2 Cor. 9:1–2; 1 Cor. 13:7).
13. Make sure your child knows exactly what is expected of him. Most of the book of Proverbs is specific counsel from a father to his son.
14. Ask his advice—include him in some of the family planning (Rom. 1:11–12; 2 Tim. 4:11; 1 Tim. 4:12; John 6:5).
15. When you make a mistake with your child, admit it and ask your child for forgiveness (Matt. 5:23–24; James 5:16).
16. Have family conferences where you discuss:
    a. Family goals
    b. Family projects
    c. Vacations
    d. Devotions
    e. Chores
    f. Discipline
    g. Complaints
    h. Suggestions
    i. Problems
    Welcome contributions from your child (Ps. 128; James 1:19; 3:13-18; Titus 1:6-8; Prov. 15:22).
17. Assess his areas of strength and then encourage him to develop them. Begin with one and encourage him to really develop in this area (2 Tim. 1:16; 4:5; 1 Pet. 4:10).
18. Give him plenty of tender loving care. Be free in your expression of love by word and deed (1 Cor. 13:1-8; 16:14; John 13:34; I Thess. 2:7–8).
19. Practice selective reinforcement. When your child does

something well, commend him. Especially let him know when his attitude and effort are what they should be (1 Thess. 1:3-10; Phil. 1:3–5; Col. 1:3–4; Eph. 1:15).

20. Be more concerned about Christian attitudes and character than you are about performance or athletic skills or clothing or external beauty or intelligence (1 Sam. 16:7; Gal. 5:22–23; 1 Pet. 3:4–5; Prov. 4:23; Matt. 23:25–28).

21. Have a lot of fun with your child. Plan to have many fun times and many special events with your child. Make a list of fun things your family can do (Ps. 128; Prov. 5:15–18; 15:13; 17:22; Eph. 6:4; Col. 3:21; Eccles. 3:4; Luke 15:22–24).

22. Help your child to learn responsibility by administering discipline fairly, consistently, lovingly, and promptly (1 Sam. 3:13; Prov. 13:24; 19:18; 22:15).

23. Look upon your child as a human *becoming* as well as a human *being*. Look upon the task of raising children as a process which takes eighteen to nineteen years to complete (Eph. 6:4; Prov. 22:6; Gal. 6:9; 1 Cor. 15:58; Isa. 28:9–10).

24. Live your convictions consistently. Your child will learn more by observing your example than he will by listening to your words (Deut. 6:4–9; 1 Thess. 2:10–12; Phil. 4:9; 1 Tim. 1:5,7).

25. Recognize that you are responsible to prepare your child for life in this world and the world to come (Eph. 6:4; Deut. 6:4–9; Ps. 78:5–7; 2 Tim. 3:15–17).

26. Be very sensitive to the needs, feelings, fears, and opinions of your child (Matt. 18:10; Col. 3:21).

27. Treat the child as though he is important to you and accepted by you (Matt. 18:5–6).

28. Avoid the use of words expressing anger or exasperation (Prov. 15:1; Eph. 4:31–32).

29. Maintain the practice of daily Bible reading, discussions, and prayer (Deut. 6:4–9; 2 Tim. 3:15; Eph. 6:4; Ps. 1:1–3; 78:5–8; 119:9, 11).

30. Become thoroughly involved as a family in a biblical church (Heb. 10:24–25; Eph. 4:11–16).

Recommended Reading

I. General Works

Jay Adams, *The Use of the Scriptures In Counseling,* Presbyterian And Reformed Publishing Company

Jay Adams, *Christian Living in the Home,* Baker Book House

Kenneth Gangel, *The Family First: Biblical Answers to Family Problems,* His International Service

Fred Hortley, *Dealing With Peer Pressure: Dare to be Different,* Fleming H. Revell Company

Marion Leach Jacobsen, *How To Keep Your Family Together and Still Have Fun,* Zondervan Publishing House

Jay Kesler, *Let's Succeed With Our Teenagers: An Encouraging Look at Parent-Teen Relations,* David C. Cook Publishing Company

C. John Miller, *Repentance And 20th Century Man,* Christian Literature Crusade

II. Resources For Sex Education In The Home

James Dobson, *Preparing For Adolescence,* Regal Books

Erwin J. Kolb, *Parent's Guide to Christian Conversation About Sex,* Concordia Publishing House

Josh McDowell and Paul Lewis, *Givers, Takers, and Other Kinds of Lovers,* Tyndale House Publishers

Josh McDowell, *Teens Speak Out: "What I Wish My Parents Knew About My Sexuality,"* Here's Life Publishers

Josh McDowell is spearheading a new nationwide campaign called "Why Wait" which will be attempting to educate parents, church leaders, and teenagers about the "adolescent sex crisis" affecting our young people. For more information on how you and your church may become involved write: Why Wait? Box 337/289 Main Place, Wheaton, Illinois 60189.

Charlie Shedd, *The Stork Is Dead,* Word Books

III. Books for Drug Education in the Home

Gordon R. McLean and Haskell Bowen, *High on the Campus: Student Drug Abuse—Is There an Answer?*, Tyndale House Publishers

R.A. Morey, *The Bible and Drug Abuse,* Presbyterian and Reformed Publishing Company

Anderson Spickard, M.D., and Barbara R. Thompson, *Dying for a Drink: What You Should Know About Alcoholism,* Word Books

Jay Strack, *Drugs and Drinking: The All American Cop-Out,* Thomas Nelson Publishers

NOTES

Chapter 1

1. *The World Almanac and Book of Facts* (New York: Pharas Books, 1987), 85.

2. Ibid.

3. Jason D. Baron, M.D., *Kids and Drugs: A Parents' Handbook of Drug Abuse, Prevention, and Treatment* (New York: GD/Perigee Books, 1983), ix.

4. Josh McDowell, *Teens Speak Out: "What I Wish My Parents Knew About My Sexuality,"* (San Bernardino: Here's Life Publishers, 1987), 14.

5. Richard Stengel, "Children Having Children," *Time,* December 9, 1985, 78–90.

6. Kathleen Cook, "A Boom in Births out of Wedlock," *USA Today,* July 17, 1987, D1.

7. "Too Soon to Tell about AIDS in Heterosexuals, Koop Says," *Washington Times,* June 19, 1987, A3.

8. McDowell, *Teens Speak Out,* 15.

9. Interview with Jerry Johnston, author of the book *Teenage Suicide.* Jerry Johnston's entire ministry is dedicated to helping prevent teenage suicide and leading people to Christ.

10. McDowell, *Teens Speak Out,* 14–15.

11. "Religion Less Critical For Today's Teens," *Miami Herald,* August 7, 1987.

12. Aurelius Augustinus, *The Confessions of St. Augustine,* trans. Edward B. Pusely, D.D. (New York: Washington Square Press, Inc., 1962), 148.

13. Ibid., 149, 173.

Chapter 2

1. Lawrence O. Richards, *Expository Dictionary of Bible Words* (Grand Rapids: Zondervan, 1985), 152–154.

2. "Public has False Impression that 1 out of 2 Marriages Fail," *Washington Times,* June 29, 1987, A5.

3. J. Allan Petersen, *The Myth of the Greener Grass* (Wheaton: Tyndale, 1983), 14.

4. Interview with Dick Purnell aired on "Truths That Transform", June 29, 1987.

5. Baron, *Kids and Drugs,* 75.

6. Phyllis York, David York, and Ted Wachtel, *Toughlove Solutions* (Garden City: Doubleday Inc., 1984), 30.

7. Benjamin Spock, M.D., *Problems of Parents,* (Westport: Greenwood Press Publishers, 1962), preface.

Chapter 3

1. Gleason L. Archer, *Encyclopedia of Bible Difficulties,* (Grand Rapids: Zondervan, 1982), 253.

2. John White, *Parents in Pain,* (Inter–Varsity, Downers Grove: Illinois, 1979), 56.

3. Jay Kesler, *Parents and Teenagers* (Wheaton: Victor Books, 1984), 261.

Chapter 4

1. Ray S. Anderson and Dennis B. Guernsey, *On Being Family: A Social Theology of the Family* (Grand Rapids: Eerdmans, 1985), 129–136.

2. Donald Sloat, *The Dangers of Growing Up in a Christian Home,* (Nashville: Thomas Nelson, 1986), 27.

Chapter 5

1. Jack Balswick and Judith Balswick, "A Theological Basis For Family Relationships," *Journal of Psychology and Christianity,* Fall (1987), 37–49.
2. Ronald L. Koteskey, "Adolescence: Unfortunate Creation of Modern Western Society," *Christian Association for Psychological Studies Bulletin,* 1981, (Vol. 7, No. 1), 25.
3. Claudia Arp, *Almost Thirteen* (Nashville: Thomas Nelson, 1986), p. 159.

Chapter 6

1. Philip G. Zimbardo, Ph.D., and Cynthia F. Hartley, M.A., "Cults Go to High School: A Theoretical and Empirical Analysis of the Initial Stage in the Recruitment Process," *Cultic Studies Journal: A Journal on Cults and Manipulative Techniques of Social Influence,* (American Family Foundation, Vol. 2, No. 2), 110.
2. Eileen Barker, *Of Gods and Men: New Religious Movements in the West,* (Macon: Mercer University Press, 1983), 312.
3. Based on conversation with staff member of Billy Graham Association.
4. Rev. Walter Debold, *Why Cults Succeed Where the Church Fails;* Ronald M. Enroth and J. Gordon Melton, *Cultic Studies Journal,* Fall/Winter (1986), 259.
5. "Which Students Are Vulnerable to Recruitment?", *Cultism On Campus,* October 1986, 2.
6. Personal Conversation between Dr. Michael D. Longone and Norman Wise.

Chapter 7

1. Dorothy Miller, Donald Miller, Fred Hofman, Robert Duggan, *Runaways: Illegal Aliens in Their Own Land* (San Francisco: Praeger, A. J. F. Bergin Publishers Book, 1980), 22, 23.

2. Ibid., 39
3. Ibid.
4. York and Wachtel, *Toughlove Solutions,* 76.

Chapter 8

1. Joseph P. Free, *Archaeology and Bible History* (Wheaton: Scripture Press Publications, Inc., 1950), 268–274).
2. Colin Chapman, *The Case for Christianity* (Grand Rapids: Eerdmans, 1983), 522.
3. Archibald Thomas Robertson, *Word Pictures in the New Testament Volume II: The Gospel According to Luke* (New York: Richard R. Smith, Inc., 1930), 209.

Chapter 9

1. Joseph Procaccini, "Parent Burnout: Latest Sign of Today's Stresses," *U.S. News and World Report,* March 7, 1983, 76, 77.

Chapter 10

1. E.S.P. Heavenor, "Commentary on Job", *The New Bible Commentary: Revised,* (Grand Rapids: Eerdmans, 1970), 424.

Chapter 11

1. Robert Coles and Geoffrey Stokes, "Sex and the American Teenager," *Christianity Today.*
2. "Building Faith: How a Child Learns to Love God," *Christianity Today,* June 13, 1986, 4I.
3. Coles and Stokes, *Christianity Today.*
4. *Christianity Today,* February 20, 1987 40–43.
5. "Characteristics of Strong Families—An Interview with Dr. Nick Stinnett," *The Christian Counselor,* Spring 1987, 1–5.

6. Gary Smalley and John Trent, Ph.D., *The Blessing* (Nashville: Thomas Nelson, 1986), 24.

Appendix III

1. Wayne A. Mack, *A Homework Manual for Biblical Counseling,* Vol. 2, *Family and Marital Problems* (Phillipsburg, New Jersey: Presbyterian and Reformed).